RETURN OF THE HOMEWORK MACHINE

Dan Gutman

PINE HILL MIDDLE SCHOOL
LIBRARY

SCHOLASTIC INC.
New York Toronto London Auckland
Sydney Mexico City New Delhi Hong Kong

No part of this publication may be reproduced, stored in a retrieval system, or transmitted in any form or by any means, electronic, mechanical, photocopying, recording, or otherwise, without written permission of the publisher. For information regarding permission, write to Simon & Schuster Books for Young Readers, an imprint of Simon & Schuster Children's Publishing Division, 1230 Avenue of the Americas, New York, NY 10020.

ISBN 978-0-545-29244-3

12 11 10 9 8 7 6 5 4 3 2 1   10 11 12 13 14 15/0

Printed in the U.S.A.   40

First Scholastic printing, September 2010

Book design by Laurent Linn
The text for this book is set in Horley Old Style.

To kids who hate homework . . .
but do it anyway

RETURN OF THE
OF THE
HOMEWORK
MACHINE

Introduction

POLICE CHIEF REBECCA FISH. GRAND CANYON. ARIZONA

Is this thing workin'? Okay. Good. We're gonna need a lotta tape for this one.

Well, remember what happened the last time with those crazy kids. It was in all the papers. Just 'bout the most exciting thing to happen 'round here since them two planes crashed over the canyon in '56.

Just to review, these four youngsters from the Grand Canyon School down the road built some machine that did their homework for 'em automatically. Smart kids. Good kids, down deep. And then, for some reason, they built themselves a catapult and chucked the whole darn contraption into the canyon. Strangest thing I ever seen.

Of course, that wouldn't be the first time

somebody did somethin' strange out here. I remember back in '93 when three people drove their cars right into the Grand Canyon after rentin' that movie *Thelma and Louise*. Fifty people died here that year all together. I think that was the record.

Must be somethin' about the canyon. That's my guess. It's the only place on the planet that opens up, you know, like a big crack. Attracts the weirdo element, you might say.

Anyhow, throwin' computers into the canyon ain't just litterin'. Those kids coulda hurt somebody. We had to bring 'em in for questionin'. You know, throw a little scare into 'em to let 'em know they did wrong.

I thought I'd seen the last of them kids. Thought we taught 'em a lesson. Guess not. 'Cause they went off and did somethin' even stupider. Only this time, somebody died.

We had to bring 'em in here again, stick 'em in separate rooms, and get their testimony on tape for the record.

Far as I'm concerned, this case is closed. Forever. I got more important things to do with my time than babysit for a bunch of nutty kids, that's for darn sure.

Chapter 1

September

SAM DAWKINS, GRADE 6

What do you want me to say? My name? Again? Don't you have it from the first time? Okay, I'm Sam Dawkins, but everybody calls me Snikwad, or Snik, on account of that's my name spelled backward. It's a snikname. Get it?

Do we really have to go through this whole thing all over again? I mean, sometimes freak accidents just happen. There's nothing you can do about it. Nobody means for them to happen. They just do. It just did. We're all sorry it happened. If any of us had known what was going to happen, we never would have done any of it. Can I go home now? I really don't like being here.

JUDY DOUGLAS, GRADE 6

I can't believe I'm sitting in this room again. I

3

want you to know that this is just the most humiliating thing that ever happened to me in my entire life. I'm not a criminal! It was an accident. We're sorry. None of us knew it was going to get out of control, I swear! I have worked so hard all my life to get good grades and sign up for lots of extracurricular activities and go to church and always do the right thing. I have been on the Principal's List every marking period since second grade. I'm not talking about the honor roll, where you can get Bs on your report card. The Principal's List! That's straight As. And now this happens . . . again! It makes me question why I try so hard to be good. I mean, really, what's the reward? If this keeps me out of the Ivy League, my mom will never let me forget it.

JUDY'S MOM

I assure you, my daughter will *never* be involved with anything like this again. Not if I have anything to say about it. I teach my children to learn from their mistakes. She is on permanent probation.

KELSEY DONNELLY. GRADE 6

We are all really sorry. I'm not just saying that because we're in trouble. We really felt terrible about what happened. It was just one of those freak accidents. Do I really have to tell the whole story from the beginning? Okay.

I have to confess, it was kinda cool seeing my picture in the paper the first time and everything. Y'know? Even if it was because we got caught heaving the homework machine into the Grand Canyon. It was even mentioned on *The Today Show*! Can you believe that? We were a little famous for a while. We had our fifteen minutes.

I mean, don't get me wrong. I felt bad and all because what we did was wrong. But you can't help but get a little tingle when you see your picture in the paper. I cut it out and put it in my scrapbook.

But this . . . this is getting old. I promise you won't see me in here again. I promise.

BRENTON DAMAGATCHI. GRADE 6

First let me say it was all my fault. The others were there, of course. But I built the machine in the first place. I have to take responsibility for anything that was done with it.

I wonder if it might be possible to invent a time machine. I have no desire to go to the past or future, personally. But if one had a time machine, anytime you made a mistake in life, you could just go back a few seconds and erase it. Just like the eraser on a pencil. Do it over. Then you would never make any mistakes. You would be perfect. Except, I suppose, for the mistakes you don't know about. You can't fix a mistake if you don't even know that you made one.

May I have a drink of water? Thanks.

RONNIE TEOTWAWKI. GRADE 6

You wanna know what I thought about the whole thing? I'll be honest. I thought it was great that Brenton, Snik, Judy, and Kelsey got caught throwing their homework machine into the canyon. What a dumb thing to do! And people always say *I* use bad judgment! It served 'em right. That's how I felt. I laughed all day.

Of course, this is a different story. I was involved. I admit it. If you need to throw me in reform school or something, well, I guess I deserve it.

MISS RASMUSSEN. FIFTH-GRADE TEACHER

They are all good kids. They really are. I felt partly responsible for the first mess because it happened on my watch. I was a first-year teacher at the time. If I had been more experienced, I probably would have noticed that their homework was so similar. I might have figured out that they were using a machine to do it for them. Ah, but you live and learn, right?

JUDY DOUGLAS. GRADE 6

You want to go all the way back to September? Okay. Well, that's my favorite time of year because the tourists have gone home. The leaves fall from the trees. It's quiet around the canyon and you don't have traffic jams and RVs all over and people everywhere with cameras and coolers. We have the Grand Canyon all to ourselves, it seems. It's like our backyard. I think we take it for granted. Sometimes I'm out with my mom in the car and we don't even look into the canyon. I've heard that people who live in New York City never even visit the Statue of Liberty. If I lived in New York, I'd be there every day!

KELSEY DONNELLY. GRADE 6

A lot of kids are here in the summer, but they're just tourists. There aren't many kids who live around here, which kinda sucks because you just see the same old faces day after day after day. It's boring. Our school is small. Everybody knows what everybody else is up to. So you do one silly thing like dye your hair and it's, like, front-page news. I bet if I lived in a big city, nobody would even notice me.

We have only one sixth-grade class, so the four of us were together again. They wouldn't let us sit together, though. Oh no, they weren't about to make *that* mistake a second time.

MR. MURPHY. SIXTH-GRADE TEACHER

It's a shame what happened. That's all I can say. Take it all the way back to the beginning? Okay.

I'm retired United States Air Force, and I worked on the space program at NASA for many years. I guess I was just drawn to the canyon, like a lot of people. You know, one of the seven wonders of the world, and all that. I used to go rafting out here on the Colorado River in my younger days.

My wife and I moved from Houston to retire, but I couldn't stand doing nothing. I started hanging around the library, researching strange things that happened at the Grand Canyon. I thought maybe I'd write a book on the topic. But

I'm the restless type. Can't sit still. So I went to school and took a few classes so I could get a teaching certificate.

The kids say I'm strict because I don't tolerate any foolishness. I suppose that's why I was hired. They wanted somebody who could keep the class in order, especially after what happened with those four. An authority figure, y'know? A military guy who would keep them in line.

But what happened, happened. I'm partly responsible, because I was there. I will never forget it. I feel deeply sorry about it.

SAM DAWKINS, GRADE 6

Mr. Murphy looked like one of those drill sergeants you see in the movies. You know, he has a crew cut you could balance a soda can on. When he walked into the class for the first time in September, I thought we'd all have to snap to attention or start marching around the playground. I was afraid he was gonna take one look at my long hair and suspend me for life.

But my dad was in the military, so I'm used to guys like that. Mr. Murphy is cool, in a way. You know where you stand with him. He doesn't say one thing and mean something else, like a lot of other guys. If he's mad, he tells you. And if you do something good, he tells you that, too.

JUDY DOUGLAS. GRADE 6

Mr. Murphy told us that he actually met Neil Armstrong, John Glenn, and all those other astronauts when he was working at NASA. Can you imagine? And here he was, teaching *us*. It was pretty neat, to think that there was just one degree of separation between me and the first man to walk on the moon.

KELSEY DONNELLY. GRADE 6

Yeah, when we came back to school in September, we knew we would have to go back to doing our homework the old-fashioned way—with pencils and papers and our brains. Ha! What a drag. I missed the homework machine. It was just so easy, sliding a work sheet into the computer and having your homework pop out of the printer a few minutes later—finished, perfect, and even in my own handwriting! Man, that was great. I'm sure Snik missed having the homework machine around too. It probably didn't matter much to Brenton and Judy one way or the other, because they're geniuses anyway. I think they actually *like* doing homework. They're freaks.

SAM DAWKINS. GRADE 6

I *still* hate homework. What a waste of time! But what are you gonna do? Kids don't rule the world. We've got no power.

MR. MURPHY. SIXTH-GRADE TEACHER

Let me see, what did we learn this year? Dividing by decimals. That was interesting. I had completely forgotten how to do it without a calculator. I had to learn all over again. I taught the kids the parts of speech too. A lot of kids have trouble with adverbs and adjectives. I like to tell them that it was a lot easier when I was their age—there were only three parts of speech back then. American history was a lot easier to memorize too, because there were only thirteen states. Sometimes the kids don't get my jokes.

SAM DAWKINS. GRADE 6

Mr. Murphy is pretty funny, for an old guy with a crew cut. He would let us joke around with him a little. But you had to be careful. If you crossed the line, he'd cut you down with a stare and let you know it was time to knock it off.

MR. MURPHY, SIXTH-GRADE TEACHER

And of course in the sixth grade, we teach about ancient civilizations—Egypt, the Aztecs, the Mayans, and the ancient Americans, too. The kids always joke that I know so much about that stuff because I lived through it. They crack me up.

JUDY DOUGLAS, GRADE 6

I found the history of the Grand Canyon to be fascinating. We think of this area as just a tourist attraction, but for more than ten thousand years, people *lived* right in the canyon! We know, because they left behind pieces of pottery, trails, and drawings carved into the rocks. The Anasazi—that's what they are called—actually grew cotton, corn, and beans here. Apparently, there was a long drought that forced them to migrate to other parts of the West. Later, the Hopi, Zuni, and Navajo Indians lived in the Grand Canyon. I went to the library to learn more about it.

KELSEY DONNELLY. GRADE 6

What a dead bore! All that ancient history stuff was such a drag. I mean, who cares whether or not people lived here a thousand years ago? What does that have to do with *us*? There were actually times when my eyelids were falling down during class.

BRENTON DAMAGATCHI. GRADE 6

I have done some of my own research, and there are people who believe that four thousand years ago an alien spacecraft crash-landed in the Grand Canyon near Comanche Point. This is true. I mean, it is true that some people believe this. It may or may not be true in reality. But anyway, the spaceship apparently was atomic-powered and used a magnetic steering system. The government found it and the craft is being hidden in a secret location. Or so they say.

MR. MURPHY. SIXTH-GRADE TEACHER

They seemed like a very nice group of young-sters to me. Very different, very interesting, each in their own way. Brenton seemed to be a real bright bulb, the kind of kid whose brain simply operated on a different, higher, level than everyone else's. A little odd, yes. But someone who looked at the world and saw things the rest of us overlooked. This is the kind of kid we were always looking for at NASA. Divergent thinkers. Judy was also very bright. She will go far. Sam was a smart one too, but he didn't want anyone to know it. One of those kids who is too cool for school, you know what I mean? Kelsey is probably a late bloomer. She hasn't come into her own yet. But she's a good judge of character. I think she has potential.

BRENTON DAMAGATCHI. GRADE 6

Late one night in September, I got an e-mail from that guy Richard Milner. He was that weird stalker who had been bothering us when we were in fifth grade. He wrote something like, "I read in the paper that you and your friends catapulted your homework machine into the canyon. I hope you picked up *all* the pieces." He was weird. I deleted the e-mail.

JUDY DOUGLAS. GRADE 6

It was around the beginning of the school year when I noticed for the first time that Brenton had a nervous habit. He would pick at the skin around his nails. He didn't *bite* his nails, like a lot of people do. He would just pick at his fingers. Usually he did it with his hands under a table or out of sight. I didn't mention it to anybody, certainly not Brenton.

He was quieter than before too. This all happened after we got caught throwing the homework machine into the canyon. I asked him if anything was bothering him, and he said no.

KELSEY DONNELLY. GRADE 6

Most people didn't even know that Brenton and Judy were boyfriend and girlfriend last summer. They were so cute together, y'know, the two brains. Two peas in a pod. I mean, they really liked each other, but at the same time they seemed completely awkward when they were together.

Snik and I were going out for a while too. It wasn't any big secret or anything. The four of us got to be pretty close during the whole homework-machine episode.

JUDY DOUGLAS. GRADE 6

In the fall, the leaves started to turn colors and drop from the trees. I thought that was a good metaphor for Brenton and I. Or is that a simile? I always get those two mixed up. Anyway, the point is that we broke up. I told Brenton it was because he seemed so nervous all the time. But the truth is that I just wasn't ready to have a boyfriend. I mean, we're only in sixth grade! We've got our whole lives ahead of us.

SAM DAWKINS. GRADE 6

Kelsey and I broke up in September, right after school started. It wasn't any big deal. I mean, we're still friends and all. I just felt strange holding hands and stuff with a girl. Guys at school were making fun of me, because Kelsey is kind of weird. Like, she used to have pink hair and stuff.

JUDY DOUGLAS. GRADE 6

Even though we weren't "going out" anymore, I think the four of us had a bond. After a year of being part of the group and everything that happened, we had . . . something. You can't go through what we did and just walk away like nothing ever happened.

Snik had become friends with Brenton because they were both obsessed with chess. And Kelsey and I had become friends too. I guess sometimes like attracts like, and sometimes opposites attract. You never know.

SAM DAWKINS. GRADE 6

I gotta admit, it was cool to be part of a group for a change. I never had a lot of friends at my old school. The kids didn't like me. I remember hearing them talk about their birthday parties, and feeling bad that I wasn't invited. My mom wanted to throw me a party, but I didn't think anybody would come, so I told her I didn't want a party. Even though I really did. I still remember that.

My birthday was coming up in October. I guess I started hinting around that Brenton, Judy, and Kelsey should get me presents. It was obnoxious, I know. But if you don't tell anybody your birthday is coming up, how are they supposed to know?

JUDY DOUGLAS. GRADE 6

One day Brenton didn't know I was looking at him, and he was picking at the skin on the side of his thumb. I mean, really picking at it to the point of making himself bleed. So even if he was not my boyfriend, he was still my friend, you know? And I pulled him aside and demanded to know what was bothering him. You don't do stuff like that to yourself unless something is bothering you, right?

At first he said nothing was wrong. But when I pointed out that his finger was bleeding, he kind of sighed and admitted something was bothering him. "What is it? What is it?" I begged. And he said, in that cryptic way of his, "Okay, I'll tell you. But not here."

Chapter 2

October

SAM DAWKINS. GRADE 6

So one day, Brenton calls this meeting. Well, that pretty much blew my mind. Brenton never calls meetings. It's not his thing. I figured he wanted to play chess. I learned the game over the last year and got pretty awesome at it, if I do say so myself. We played a lot over the summer. I even beat him a few times, which was amazing. Me, beating super genius Brenton Damagatchi! What a rush!

KELSEY DONNELLY. GRADE 6

I thought Brenton called the meeting to tell us that he rebuilt the homework machine. That would have been great, because I was having a tough time in school. Mr. Murphy is much harder than Miss Rasmussen was, and sixth grade is a lot harder than fifth. Homework was such a drag, anyway.

JUDY DOUGLAS. GRADE 6

I assumed that Brenton had some deep, dark secret to tell us. I was almost afraid to find out what it was. I remember thinking, *What if he had murdered somebody?* Can you imagine?

Well, whatever it was, I was glad we had the meeting. Because the four of us hadn't been hanging out much since the summer, and I missed them. I missed being part of a group. They were my friends.

BRENTON'S MOM

I hadn't seen Brenton's friends for some time, so I was a little bit shocked when they showed up at the door after school one day. I had mixed feelings about it, to be honest with you. I felt that they were a bad influence on Brenton, especially that boy Sam, and Kelsey. She had pink hair! My son never would have gotten into any trouble if not for those kids, I'm certain of that.

But there comes an age when you can't pick and choose your children's friends for them. You have to leave it up to them, and hope they use good judgment. I baked them some brownies and left them alone. But I kept Brenton's door open, just in case.

BRENTON DAMAGATCHI. GRADE 6

Something had been bothering me ever since the day we got called into the sheriff's office last June. No, even before that. I reminded the others about the little blinking red light on the homework machine. When we were using it, one day I noticed that the light was still blinking even after I had turned the computer off. I didn't think much of it at the time. Then, when we finally pulled the plug so we could throw the whole thing into the Grand Canyon, the little red light was *still* blinking. There was no traditional power source at all, but the light was on. No battery. The chip that controlled that light had somehow figured out—on its own—how to power itself. It was like it had a mind of its own.

KELSEY DONNELLY. GRADE 6

Brenton went on and on about some stupid red light on the computer. I didn't see the point. So what? The light stayed on. Big deal. Maybe it was a glow-in-the-dark light or something.

BRENTON DAMAGATCHI. GRADE 6

The thing is, after those hikers found the busted-up homework machine near the bottom of the Grand Canyon, we got called back here like we are now. The sheriff had a trash bag full of computer parts that had been found. I looked through the stuff carefully, and found just about every part of my old computer. Except one. The little blinking red light. It was missing. The brain of the whole thing was missing.

SAM DAWKINS. GRADE 6

I just about busted up laughing. Poor Brenton was losing sleep over some stupid little computer part that wasn't with the other junk they found at the bottom of the canyon. Can you believe that? The guy's gonna have a heart attack some day. You can't sweat the small stuff like that. I told him to take a chill pill.

JUDY DOUGLAS. GRADE 6

I thought Brenton was overreacting some-what. He is a worrier, like me. But even I didn't care about some silly little light. Okay, so they didn't recover every single piece of the computer. That's not so unusual. There was probably debris scattered over a wide area after it hit the rocks. We told Brenton there was nothing to worry about. The light probably got washed away by the Colorado River, or maybe it's still out there, buried in the mud. The point was that it was harmless.

KELSEY DONNELLY. GRADE 6
After the big meeting was over, we played Ping-Pong. I beat Judy. She totally can't hit a backhand.

BRENTON DAMAGATCHI. GRADE 6
After they left, I checked my e-mail, like I do about ten times a day. There was a note from that Milner guy. All he wrote was, "Did you find the chip?"

MR. MURPHY. SIXTH-GRADE TEACHER
One of the important parts of the sixth-grade curriculum here is the Anasazi. They were people who lived in this part of the country two thousand years ago. They were the ancestors of the Indian tribes, like the Hopi, Zuni, and Pueblo. In fact, the word "Anasazi" means "enemy ancestors" in the Navajo language.

JUDY DOUGLAS. GRADE 6
Mr. Murphy told us all about the Anasazi. Who would have thought that anybody ever lived

right inside the Grand Canyon? Of course, the canyon wasn't as deep as it is now. But the Anasazi farmed, and they built dwellings out of mud and stone. And then, around 1300 A.D., they left. Nobody really knows why. It's a mystery. I found the whole thing to be really quite interesting. Mr. Murphy is an expert in history and space and . . . just about everything. He knows so much!

MR. MURPHY. SIXTH-GRADE TEACHER

I didn't know anything about the Anasazi. The kids don't realize this, but every week, I go to the library and research whatever we are studying the next week. You have to keep one step ahead of those little munchkins, you know?

One day, Judy came to the library while I was there. She was looking for information about the Anasazi. That's the mark of a dedicated student! I had to pretend I wasn't reading the material for the first time.

KELSEY DONNELLY. GRADE 6

Learning about those cliff-dweller people was a big bore, like everything else in school. I guess kids in Texas are forced to learn about cowboys, and kids in Hawaii are forced to learn about pineapples, and kids in Pennsylvania are forced to learn about . . . gee, I don't know. Pencils? But we happen to live in Arizona, so they force us to learn about a bunch of people who made mud houses. What I want to know is, if those Anasazi people were so important, how come kids in Texas, Hawaii, and Pennsylvania don't have to learn about them?

SAM DAWKINS. GRADE 6

Mr. Murphy said those Anasazi dudes built some of their houses right into the cliffs. What's up with *that*? Who would want to live on a cliff? What if you were sleeping and in the middle of the night you rolled over? You might fall off the cliff. That would really suck. No wonder their civilization collapsed. They probably fell off the cliffs and died. Nothing mysterious about that.

JUDY DOUGLAS. GRADE 6

I was at the library one day looking things up. They have every issue of the *Phoenix Gazette* going back over a hundred years, and it's fun to look at the old ads and things. Anyway, I stumbled across an article from 1909. It said that an entire Egyptian city had been found in the Grand Canyon! No kidding. According to the article, this city had hundreds of rooms, artifacts, hieroglyph-ics, and even mummies. Mr. Murphy was there that day, and I showed it to him.

EXPLORATIONS IN GRAND CANYON

Mysteries of Immense Rich Cavern Being Brought to Light

JORDAN IS ENTHUSED

Remarkable Finds Indicate Ancient People Migrated From Orient

The latest news of the progress of the explorations of what is now regarded by scientists as not only the oldest archaeo-logical discovery in the United States, but one of the most valuable in the world, which was mentioned some time ago in the Gazette, was brought to the city by G.E. Kinkaid, the explorer who found this great underground citadel of the Grand Canyon during a trip from Green River, Wyoming, down the Colorado river, in a wooden boat, to Yuma, several months ago. According to the story related to the Gazette, the archaeologists of the Smithsonian Institute, which is financing the explorations, have made discoveries which almost conclusively prove that the race which inhabited this mysterious cavern, hewn in solid rock by human hands, was of oriental origin, possibly from Egypt, tracing back to Rameses. If their theories are born out by the translation of the tablets engraved with hieroglyphics, the mystery of the prehistoric peoples of North America, their ancient arts, who they were and whence they came, will be solved. Egypt and the Nile, and Arizona and the Colorado will be linked by a historical chain running back to ages which stagger the wildest fancy of the fictionist.

MR. MURPHY, SIXTH-GRADE TEACHER

Judy showed me this article about an Egyptian city in the Grand Canyon. This caught my eye, because I'd never heard of such a thing. I had been taught that all Native Americans were descended from Ice Age explorers who came across from Asia on the Bering Strait. But this article suggested people came from Egypt to the Grand Canyon.

Unfortunately, I didn't have time to look into it. There were papers to grade, tests to write, lesson plans to work out. But I made a copy of the article so I could look into it later.

SAM DAWKINS. GRADE 6

All summer long, Brenton and I played a ton of chess. Like every day. I mean, there were days when we wouldn't even stop to eat. But somewhere along the line, I lost interest. It's a cool game and all, but even a good thing gets old after a while.

JUDY DOUGLAS. GRADE 6

That was another thing that bothered me. Brenton was supposed to be my boyfriend, but all he ever wanted to do was play chess with Snik. I hardly ever saw him over the summer.

Personally, I have a problem with the whole idea of chess, I must confess. I know it is a real intellectual game, but I can't get past the idea that it's a simulation of warfare. Two armies lined up against each other. Capturing enemy soldiers. Violence. Doesn't a game like that just promote aggressive behavior, like violent video games and movies?

SAM DAWKINS. GRADE 6

I told Judy I was gonna invent a new kind of chess game. Instead of two armies that try to kill each other, you have two armies that compete to make the most friends. And then at the end of the game, everybody holds hands and sways back and forth while they sing "Kumbaya." She told me to shut up. I swear, that girl has no sense of humor.

JUDY DOUGLAS. GRADE 6

Don't tell him I said this, but my theory is that Snik stopped playing chess because it reminded him of his dad. *He* was the one who taught Snik how to play, and when he was sent to Iraq they played chess by e-mail. When Snik's dad was killed in the war, it had to affect him.

BRENTON DAMAGATCHI. GRADE 6

Why did Snik stop playing chess? My theory is that the human brain is very adaptable. Like, when you first jump into a pool, the water always feels cold. But after a few minutes of swimming, you don't feel cold anymore. And when you eat something that you really love, the first bite tastes better than the tenth bite. We adapt to things.

What does that have to do with chess? Well, Snik adapted to the fun of the game. In the beginning, it was all new and exciting to him. But he got used to it. Once the novelty was gone, he was ready to move on to something else.

MR. MURPHY. SIXTH-GRADE TEACHER

No, I never liked chess. I know it's a military simulation, and a lot of the guys I was with in the service played it. But I've seen war with my own eyes. I saw my own men die. War is about blood and death. Fear and confusion. Killing people who hate you and want to kill you even though they've never met you. It's not about jumping around squares with little plastic figures.

KELSEY DONNELLY. GRADE 6

After they gave up chess, the boys got obsessed with model rocketry, of all things. The whole rocket stuff started because Snik had been hinting up and down about his birthday coming up. I thought it would be cool to throw him a surprise party. Judy and Brenton liked the idea, and we got Snik's mom in on it. She sent him out on some lame errand, and when he came back home, we jumped out from behind the curtains and freaked him out. It was cool. Mrs. Dawkins made a cake and we sang "Happy Birthday," and Snik blew out the candles. It was cute. He looked like such a little boy while he was opening his presents. I got him some video game where you get to shoot and kill everything

29

in sight. I knew he'd like it because there was a warning label on the package that said it was inappropriate for kids.

JUDY DOUGLAS. GRADE 6

I bought him a book on the history of graphic novels. Snik always says that he hates to read, but I know that he reads comic books, so I thought he would want to learn more about them.

BRENTON DAMAGATCHI. GRADE 6

There's a hobby shop in Williams that I go to sometimes with my mom. They have a lot of model trains, cars, planes, stuff like that. I was in there one day when I noticed a shelf filled with model rockets. That seemed like the kind of thing Snik might like, so I got him one for his birthday present. In retrospect, it was not a wise choice.

SAM DAWKINS. GRADE 6

Of all the presents I got, the coolest one was the rocket. It was called "Pop Fly" and it was made by a company called Estes. The thing was about two feet tall, and it was shaped like a baseball bat. The best thing was that at the top of the rocket was a baseball. So you shoot the thing up three hundred feet in the air, and when it reaches its highest point, the baseball separates from the rest of the rocket. Then you try to catch the ball when it comes down. Way cool!

BRENTON DAMAGATCHI. GRADE 6

I used to have a few of these model rockets myself. They have a small engine with propellant inside. You ignite it with an electrical spark. The rocket goes up, and its body is made of a few hollow pieces. You insert a little parachute between the payload section and the body tube. So once the propellant is all used up, an ejection charge blows the tubes apart. They're connected by a rubber shock cord. The whole thing floats back down and you can put it together and use it again with a new engine. It's quite ingenious.

KELSEY DONNELLY. GRADE 6

Snik and Brenton put the baseball rocket together from the kit. We all went out to the field near the school to shoot it off. Judy's dad had a bunch of baseball gloves, so we each took one to try and catch the ball when it came down. We chipped in a dollar each, and whoever caught the ball would get to keep four dollars. Like *I'm* gonna catch a ball, right? We all had to move fifteen feet away from the rocket. Me and Judy pretty much just watched and covered our heads with the baseball gloves.

SAM DAWKINS. GRADE 6

So me and Brenton put the rocket together real carefully. I put the decals on the outside. It looked awesome. You have to pack this flame-resistant stuff called wadding around the parachute so it doesn't burn when the ejection charge goes off. Brenton had an old launch rod we used so the rocket would go straight up in the air instead of at some crazy angle. We all got out of the way and put on baseball gloves. Everybody did the countdown. Ten . . . nine . . . eight . . . you know. I pushed the button on the controller to send the spark along the wire that would ignite the engine.

And you know what happened? The thing just blew up on the launch pad! *Pow!* It didn't go anywhere. I mean, it just disintegrated.

The girls freaked out, but Brenton and I were laughing our heads off. It was a riot. Brenton spent like seventeen dollars of his own money on this rocket, and it just exploded in a tenth of a second. It was still cool, though. I love watching stuff blow up too. I decided right away to get another rocket and figure out what went wrong.

BRENTON DAMAGATCHI. GRADE 6

There was an electrical malfunction of some sort. I'm not exactly sure what transpired. Maybe we got a wire crossed in the controller, or the engine was upside-down or something.

JUDY DOUGLAS. GRADE 6

I couldn't believe they thought it was funny when the rocket blew up. Boys can be so immature. To be honest, I don't like the whole idea of shooting rockets up in the air. Mr. Murphy told us the main reason the United States started a space program in the first place wasn't to explore outer space. No, the main reason was to land a man on the moon before the Russians did.

Isn't that silly and immature? We spent billions and billions of dollars to go to the moon so we could win some symbolic military victory. It was like a sport.

Don't boys ever do anything that doesn't involve one side winning and the other side losing? I think the world would be a lot better if women ran things.

MR. MURPHY. SIXTH-GRADE TEACHER

One day in language arts, I assigned the class to write a one-page "what if" essay. That's an essay in which you speculate how the world would be different if something was changed. Judy turned in an excellent essay. I have it here in my briefcase. . . .

WHAT IF WOMEN RAN THE WORLD?

by Judy Douglas

If women ran the world, there would be no more war. Because if mothers were in charge of the military, nobody would ever send their son or daughter off to fight.

Women are more caring and sensitive than

34

men. If women ran the world, poor people would no longer go hungry because we would make sure to feed them. We would take all the extra food we throw away at restaurants and super-markets, so homeless people would get three meals a day. We would feed the hungry, clothe the poor, and shelter the homeless. We would stop polluting the atmosphere and put an end to global warming.

If women ran the world, there would be less crime, and more compassion. Less hate, more love. Less fighting, more cooperation. People would respect one another and obey the law. There would be less smoking and drinking and drug abuse too. The world would be a bet-ter, safer, happier place. Everything would be a lot cleaner and neater too. Because most boys are pigs.

JUDY DOUGLAS. GRADE 6

Mr. Murphy liked my essay a lot, and he even read it out loud to the class. So then, of course, the next day, Snik came in with his stupid essay.

WHAT IF WOMEN RAN THE WORLD?

by Sam Dawkins

If women ran the world, it would be horrible. Toilet seats would be down all the time. They would probably cancel the Super Bowl and replace it with some lame ice-skating show. There would be no more heavy-metal music, and hip-hop would be so boring.

If women ran the world, we would have to hug each other all the time. You could never drink anything out of a bottle anymore. You'd have to pour your drink into a cup for no good reason. And if you put the cup down on the table without a coaster, they'd probably throw you in jail for life. Guys would be put in prison for wiping their nose on their sleeve. Forget about spitting anywhere. We would have to swallow our saliva, which is way more disgusting than spitting it out. You wouldn't be allowed to wear T-shirts and jeans anymore. Everybody would have to get dressed up nicely all the time. We'd spend hours fussing with our hair and spend every weekend visiting relatives. There would be no more cool cars. They would probably ban paintball, professional wrestling, NASCAR, and anything else that's cool. We'd have to sit around and drink tea and bow to each other. Nothing good would ever be on TV. You'd flip through the channels and it would be all soap operas and cooking shows. All movies would be musicals, with dancing, and everybody would end happily ever after with a couple kissing and walking off into the sunset. The only thing you could talk about would be how much you weigh.

MR. MURPHY. SIXTH-GRADE TEACHER

What could I do? I gave both of them an A.

Anyway, Halloween was coming up, and I wanted it to be more than just the usual candy grab. So I assigned the class to pick a costume that had something to do with flying or aviation or the space program. They had to research it and give an oral report, in costume, on Halloween.

BRENTON DAMAGATCHI. GRADE 6

I dressed up like Wernher von Braun. He was a German rocket scientist who was brought to the United States after World War II. He joined NASA and helped design the Saturn V rocket. We probably never would have reached the moon if it hadn't been for Wernher von Braun. Some people call him the father of the United States space program.

It occurred to me that if aliens from outer space were ever to come to Earth, the best time to do it would be Halloween because all the humans are dressed up in weird costumes and nobody would notice the aliens. They wouldn't even need disguises.

JUDY DOUGLAS. GRADE 6

I dressed up like Sally Ride. In 1983, she became the first American woman in outer space. She also helped develop the robot arm they used on the space shuttle.

We can't do much trick-or-treating around here, because there aren't many houses. So we had a Halloween party at school and everybody brought candy. It's not quite the same as going door to door, but it's fun and better than nothing. I don't like to eat too much candy anyway, because it is fattening and bad for your teeth.

SAM DAWKINS. GRADE 6

I dressed up in a squirrel monkey costume.

Everybody was all mad because they said monkeys don't have anything to do with space. But I told them that before people were sent up in orbit, we sent up a bunch of monkeys to see if they could survive. Some of them died, but this monkey named Baker was one of the first living creatures to go to space and come back to Earth safely. So I dressed up like Baker for Halloween. Ha!

I looked all this stuff up. Baker actually lived to be twenty-seven years old, and he's buried at the U.S. Space and Rocket Center in Huntsville, Alabama.

Okay, I admit it. I just wanted to dress up like a monkey. What's wrong with that? Why does everything have to be a learning experience, anyway? Can't we just have fun at school once in a while?

KELSEY DONNELLY. GRADE 6

I dressed up like a witch. I dress up like a witch *every* Halloween, and I wasn't about to change this year. Mr. Murphy was going to give me a bad grade because he said I ignored the assignment. But I told him that witches fly on broomsticks, so technically my costume did have something to do with aviation.

MR. MURPHY. SIXTH-GRADE TEACHER

What could I do? I gave out As to kids who dressed up like witches and monkeys.

Chapter 3

November

BRENTON DAMAGATCHI. GRADE 6

I couldn't stop thinking about the blinking light and the chip that controlled it. It was still out there somewhere. That Milner guy kept e-mailing me and asking if I had found it yet. I didn't like that guy.

SAM DAWKINS. GRADE 6

I bought another Estes rocket called Blue Ninja. It was beautiful, around thirty inches tall, with a D engine, and colored fins and nose cone. Brenton and I put it together real carefully, making sure all the electrical stuff was in right this time. Then we took it out to the field and set it up. We did the countdown, I pushed the button, and the thing shot up like . . . like a rocket! I mean, it went up perfectly. I don't know exactly how high it got, but the box said 780 feet.

Then, just like it said on the box, the parachute popped out and the rocket floated back down to us. Oh man, that was a beautiful sight! We were all yelling and screaming, like we had won the lottery or something. Way cool. I was hooked on model rockets.

MR. MURPHY. SIXTH-GRADE TEACHER

I was thrilled when the kids came in and told me about Sam's model rocket. Boys like Sam need a passion in life they can get excited about. Otherwise, they get into trouble. And rocketry is an excellent hobby. That's what I did when I was a kid, and it took me all the way to a career at NASA.

This was one of those magical "teachable moments." I could use their interest in rocketry to teach them about electricity, geometry, math, physics, earth science, weather, the environment, you name it. It's always good to sneak in a little learning when the kids least expect it.

KELSEY DONNELLY. GRADE 6

Yeah, shooting stuff up in the air is cool.

JUDY DOUGLAS. GRADE 6

Mr. Murphy started a rocketry club at school. Snik and Brenton were the only ones who signed up, and the principal said you need at least three participants to have a club. So Kelsey and I signed up too, even though, as I said before, I have mixed feelings about rockets. I just wanted the boys to have their club.

I must admit it was pretty neat watching the rocket launch. You have to be really careful, though. The boys didn't want to read the safety warnings, but I did. When you launch a rocket, everybody has to back away a certain number of feet, depending on the power of the engine. You need to have a blast deflector to prevent the exhaust from hitting the ground. I never realized the countdown had a purpose. You do it to make sure everyone is paying attention. And if the engine fails or misfires, you're supposed to remove the safety interlock, disconnect the battery, and wait sixty seconds before you approach the rocket. It's surprisingly complicated.

SAM DAWKINS. GRADE 6

I have this bank account where I keep birthday

money that was given to me by my grandparents and stuff. There was almost a thousand bucks in it. My mom said I could use some of the money to buy rocket gear. So I bought some more rockets, launchers, extra engines, and some other stuff I knew I would need.

MR. MURPHY. SIXTH-GRADE TEACHER

In my day, the idea of launching a rocket was strictly government business. It was very difficult to build a homemade rocket. But now, plain old citizens all over the world are building very sophisticated rockets and launching them on their own. It is actually possible to shoot something out of the Earth's atmosphere.

JUDY DOUGLAS. GRADE 6

One day at school, Kelsey showed up with a pink T-shirt that said, "Polar Bears Are People Too." There was a picture of a bear hanging onto a little ice floe. I told her it was cute. She told me she saw some documentary about the environment the night before and it changed her life.

KELSEY DONNELLY. GRADE 6

Did you know that we burn twenty million barrels of oil a day? Every day! And what do you think happens to it after it's burned? It turns into carbon dioxide, which is trapped by the atmosphere. Which is getting hotter and hotter each year. Glaciers are melting. Species are becoming extinct. We're going to make this planet uninhabitable, and nobody even cares. Why aren't we doing anything about this? The world is coming to an end and all kids care about is who Brittney Spears and Lindsey Lohan are going out with. It's ridiculous.

JUDY DOUGLAS. GRADE 6

She went on and on about the melting icecaps, stranded polar bears, greenhouse gases, and all that stuff. I care about the environment too, of course. Everybody does. We recycle. But Kelsey always goes to the extreme. She is such an alarmist. I mean, really! I'm sure that if the world was really coming to an end, the world leaders would get together and do something about it.

KELSEY DONNELLY. GRADE 6

I would never say this to her face, but Judy can

be a little selfish and narrow-minded sometimes. Her biggest concern always seems to be getting into law school someday, and her own future. Maybe she should spend a little more time thinking about the future of the human race.

SAM DAWKINS. GRADE 6

I thought it was a riot. Kelsey is always into weird stuff that will attract attention to her. One day she comes in with pink hair or a pierced belly button, and the next day, out of nowhere, she says she's a tree hugger. And then the day after that, she forgot all about it. She cracks me up. You never know what she's gonna be into next.

KELSEY DONNELLY. GRADE 6

Yeah, they made fun of me. Kids have always made fun of me. And you know what? I don't care. I used to care, when I was little. But after a while you have to stand up for what you believe in. I think it is entirely possible that the world is going to come to an end in my lifetime, or my children's lifetime. What a horrifying thought.

SAM DAWKINS. GRADE 6

Kelsey was telling us her doomsday scenario

about the world coming to an end and all this stuff. She was so serious, but it was hard to keep a straight face. So I looked over at Brenton and he looked at me, and he's got this sly grin on his face and a gleam in his eye and I know what he's thinking and he knows what I'm thinking and the rest, well, you know what happened.

JUDY DOUGLAS. GRADE 6

Remember Red Socks Day? It was the day after Brenton got on the Internet and spread around this message that everybody should wear red socks to school. Sure enough, the next day, just about every boy and girl in America wore red socks to school. It was pretty amazing. Anyway, when Kelsey was talking about the end of the world, Brenton and Snik got this screwy idea in their head that it would be a funny prank to invent a fake doomsday cult. I told them it was a bad idea, and they were hurting Kelsey's feelings. But did the boys listen? No, of course not. They're boys.

KELSEY DONNELLY. GRADE 6

The boys got all excited about this stupid idea of seeing how many suckers would believe the end of the world was coming. At first I was offended, because they were making fun of me and not taking my ideas seriously. But then I just decided that they were silly and immature, which is what boys are.

BRENTON DAMAGATCHI. GRADE 6

We thought it would be cool to start a cult of nutballs who worship the Grand Canyon. Life began there millions of years ago, we decided, when aliens landed and creatures from the center of the earth came up through the crack in the surface to mate with them. That's how the human race started. We decided to name this philosophy "Canyonism." I started working up a Canyonism website.

SAM DAWKINS. GRADE 6

I wanted to call it "Brentonism," but he didn't want his name in it. Brenton is so modest! We worked out all the details of this bogus cult. We decided that Canyonists worship a mysterious genius named Notnerb, which is just Brenton backward. Notnerb performs miracles, and if you pray to him, he'll reward you with frequent-flyer miles and other awesome prizes. Just like a game show. And if you don't want the prizes, you can lose weight instead. That's what people want in life, right? To have more stuff or to lose weight.

Anyway, we decided that Canyonists can achieve immortality if they stand on their heads and become one with the earth. And everybody has to eat one Hostess Twinkie every day to advance to the afterlife. And it's a sin to eat pretzels on Wednesday. It was just stupid stuff, you know? Oh, and the world is going to end on Mother's Day for everyone except the people who are in the Grand Canyon. They'll be protected.

Brenton and I were laughing our heads off.

BRENTON DAMAGATCHI, GRADE 6

The website was up just a few minutes when I got an IM from some guy in Ohio who wanted to become a Canyonist. He said he had been searching his whole life for something to believe in, and that Canyonism was the first thing he'd seen that made sense. He wanted to send us money and everything. It was just sad and pathetic that anyone would take such a thing seriously. But soon, the website had hundreds of hits. People are crazy.

POLICE CHIEF REBECCA FISH

It was 'round about the end of November, I reckon, when I found a white male runaway wanderin' 'round Grand Canyon Village. About twenty years of age. Said he worshiped the Grand Canyon. The kid kept trying to stand on his head and pray to somebody named Notnerb. Wasn't makin' any sense at all. Figured he was high on somethin'. We put him on a bus headin' back east. I tell you, we get all kinds of loonies here so I didn't think much of it. The kid had a backpack filled with Twinkies.

BRENTON DAMACATCHI. GRADE 6

A couple of days after the website went up online, I got another e-mail from that Milner guy. He went on and on about Canyonism and what a brilliant idea it was. He wanted to team up or something and promised me there were millions of dollars to be made from Canyonism. He wanted to print books, make videos, and sell souvenirs to saps who bought into the idea.

I didn't like Milner. I didn't like what he was suggesting we do. I pulled down the website. Maybe I should have changed my e-mail address so he would stop bothering me.

JUDY DOUGLAS. GRADE 6

Richard Milner was this strange man who somehow found out about the homework machine while we were using it. He pestered us for a long time about it. It was almost like stalking. I wanted to call the police on him, but the others talked me out of it.

SAM DAWKINS. GRADE 6

Personally, I thought Milner was harmless. He just wanted to make money. Nothing wrong with that. It's America, right? We all want to get rich or die trying. But the others were so freaked out by the guy. Especially Brenton. He was really spooked.

POLICE CHIEF REBECCA FISH

Day after Thanksgiving, one of our copters spotted somebody wanderin' around the canyon, near the same spot where them kids chucked the computer. Went down to check it out, and it turned out to be that Damagatchi boy. Bright kid, but a little strange if you ask me. Wouldn't tell me what he was doin' down there. But it was late in the day and the boy didn't have enough water with him. I was afraid he might not be able to get back up before dark, so I brought him out.

Every year a bunch of tourists need to be rescued, but it's usually not the local yokels. I just figured it's kids doing stupid things. Boys will be boys.

JUDY DOUGLAS. GRADE 6

I became very concerned when we heard that Brenton was wandering around the canyon and the police had to rescue him. It's just not like him to be irrational. They say there's a thin line between genius and madness. I was wondering if maybe Brenton was crossing the line.

SAM DAWKINS. GRADE 6

All geniuses are a little nuts, right? Brenton once told me that thousands of years ago, an alien spaceship crash-landed in the Grand Canyon. He read about it on the Internet, and he really thought it might be true. I figured he was looking for the spaceship. Why else would he be hiking down there with no water at the end of November?

KELSEY DONNELLY. GRADE 6

Judy was so worried about Brenton that she

said we had to have an "intervention." Man, I didn't even know what that meant! So we all went over to Snik's house after school. I figured that Brenton just went off the deep end.

SAM DAWKINS. GRADE 6

I asked Brenton if he was searching for an alien spaceship and he said no. He said he was looking for that little red light from the homework machine. I couldn't believe it! That stupid light! He was obsessed with it! We all told him to get over it. But that's when Brenton dropped his little bombshell on us.

BRENTON DAMAGATCHI. GRADE 6

I felt that I needed to tell them the truth. The reason the homework machine was so powerful was because its CPU was a "superchip" I bought at a computer flea market in Williams. That chip was what kept the little red light on. The man who sold me the chip in the first place, I finally realized, was that guy Richard Milner.

SAM DAWKINS. GRADE 6

Brenton told us he was pretty sure that the guy who sold him the computer chip was Milner, and that Milner got it from some gangsters in Japan or someplace. Apparently, Milner didn't have the technical know-how to do anything with the chip himself, so he found a smart kid who did— Brenton. Then he started watching what Brenton did with it.

JUDY DOUGLAS. GRADE 6

I didn't quite understand it, but that computer chip was some kind of cutting-edge technology that nobody else in the world had yet. It was super fast, and it could do things normal computer chips couldn't—like work with no source of power. It was probably stolen from the company that developed it. If it fell into the wrong hands, well, who knows what might happen? We all realized at once that we had to find that chip. And we couldn't let anybody know.

KELSEY DONNELLY. GRADE 6

It was starting to get cold out, and soon there would be snow on the ground. So we had to move fast. That night, all of us snuck out of our houses at two o'clock in the morning. We had to do it in the dark because that would be the only way we'd be able to see the blinking red light. Snik had a metal detector. The rest of us brought flashlights.

It was exciting. We hiked down until we found the spot where the homework machine landed. We spent about an hour down there, searching on our hands and knees. But we never found the stupid light, or the stupid chip.

Chapter 4

December

RONNIE TEOTWAWKI. GRADE 6

Of course they couldn't find the chip. I had it. As soon as I heard on the news that they catapulted their homework machine into the canyon, I hiked down there to see if I could find it. The police had cleaned up most of the mess, but there were still some pieces scattered around the rocks. When I saw that little red light blinking, I had a hunch that I hit the jackpot.

I knew there had to be something special about that computer. You can't take just any old PC and program it to do homework. Even Brenton isn't *that* smart. The computer had to have some kind of special chip inside it, a superchip.

Everybody thinks I'm dumb because I don't do good in school. But I know how to build a computer. I built one from a kit when I was nine, and I built one from scratch last year. When I found their chip, I knew I could use it to build my *own* homework machine. And I wasn't gonna share it with anybody.

BRENTON DAMAGATCHI. GRADE 6

Ronnie and I were in a computer class together back when we were in third grade. It was one of those after-school programs. He had a knack for rewiring circuit boards. I thought that we might become friends because we had this common interest. But we didn't get along, so I stayed away from him.

JUDY DOUGLAS. GRADE 6

Brenton was really miserable when we couldn't find the little red light. We didn't know what to do to cheer him up.

BRENTON DAMAGATCHI. GRADE 6

Milner's e-mails were getting weirder. He started ranting about how technology can be used for both good and bad purposes. Like the invention of the airplane, for instance. It can be used to airlift medical supplies to victims of an earthquake. But it can also be used to drop an atomic bomb. He was right, of course, but I was starting to think Milner was crazy. He always ended his e-mails with the words, "Did you find the chip yet?"

SAM DAWKINS, GRADE 6

I knew what would get Brenton's mind off that stupid blinking red light—shooting up a cool rocket! So I went online and ordered the Estes CC Express. It's a Level 2 rocket, and we had to spend a long time putting it together. But this thing could *fly*—1,790 feet. That's because it's a two-stage rocket, with two D engines. It is a beautiful thing. Two feet high. Red with a black tip. We shot that baby up after school one day, and it looked like it was never coming down. I thought it might leave the Earth's atmosphere. Mr. Murphy even came out to see the launch.

MR. MURPHY, SIXTH-GRADE TEACHER

I was impressed. The boys had done an excellent job putting together the rocket. It wasn't one of these quickie cut-and-paste jobs, like I have seen some kids build. They were very careful to cut, sand, and attach the fins so the rocket would fly straight. They really got the maximum height out of it. I told them I was proud of them.

BRENTON DAMAGATCHI. GRADE 6

I did some research and discovered that by adding a few chemicals, I could double the power of the engines and double the maximum height of the rocket. Mr. Murphy helped me.

SAM DAWKINS. GRADE 6

Mr. Murphy told us we better watch out, because rocket people are a lot like boat people. He said that people who are into boats usually start out with a little dinghy not much bigger than a rowboat. And then, right away, they want a bigger one with a stronger engine so they can go faster and farther. Soon, they outgrow that and they start looking around for something bigger. Once they buy *that* boat, it starts looking small and they want a *bigger* one. And the next thing they know, they're sinking their whole life savings into a yacht or whatever. I told Mr. Murphy he was nuts. We were just having some fun with rockets.

JUDY DOUGLAS. GRADE 6

We started doing heavy math stuff with decimals and fractions this year. Up until now, math came really easy to me. Addition, subtraction, multiplication, and division gave me no problems at all. But when you have to divide something like 54.369 by 1.731 or convert decimals into fractions, that's hard! I really wished I had the homework machine sometimes to help me.

RONNIE TEOTWAWKI. GRADE 6

So I took Brenton's superchip and cleaned it off really good. It still had the wire attached to that little red light, so I had to be careful with it. The chip had a standard input. I opened my computer up and installed the chip into one of the open slots.

Building my own homework machine wasn't as hard as I thought it was gonna be. I had to buy a scanner because my printer can't do that. But once I had them both hooked up, it was easy to train the computer to recognize my handwriting and voice. I programmed the computer to search the Internet for just about anything. With all that in place, it was simple to slip a worksheet into the scanner, tell the computer to read the questions, go online to find the answers, and print them out in my handwriting. Brenton isn't the only smart kid in the world.

MR. MURPHY, SIXTH-GRADE TEACHER

I had been warned about Ronnie. The reports on him said he was a troublemaker. I remember when I walked into the class on the first day of school, all the other kids were sitting very politely, with their hands folded. But Ronnie was leaning back in his chair with his feet up on the desk. It wasn't a big deal, but it showed disrespect. He was sending me a signal that he wouldn't meekly submit to a teacher's authority.

I must admit that I was a little surprised in December when his homework grades shot up to As. I didn't think much of it at the time. It never occurred to me that he might be cheating. I just thought he had turned over a new leaf. I believe all kids are good deep down inside.

JUDY DOUGLAS, GRADE 6

Mr. Murphy handed back our homework one day. I only got a 96 because I wrote that John

Glenn was the first American in space, but actually it was Alan Shepard. A careless mistake, but it was still an A.

Anyway, Ronnie was sitting next to me. Usually I didn't pay attention to him because I thought he was just a mean boy who was surely going to end up in jail someday. But I happened to glance to my right just as Mr. Murphy handed Ronnie his paper and I saw that he got 100. My eyes must have bugged out or something, because Ronnie smirked at me and made some remark about getting a higher grade than I did.

RONNIE TEOTWAWKI. GRADE 6

Ha! Once I had a homework machine of my own, I didn't have to waste my nights doing that crap anymore. I could kick back, watch TV, and play *Grand Theft Auto* all night. It was great.

But the best part about finding that chip was being able to stick it to the smart kids. Judy and Brenton and some of the others thought they were so great because they like school and the teachers all think they're so perfect. I wish I had a picture of Judy's face when she saw that I got a better mark on my homework than she did.

SAM DAWKINS. GRADE 6

I was suspicious of Ronnie right away. There's no way a pre–juvenile delinquent like him is gonna go from Ds to As just like that. Brenton and I talked it over. It was Brenton who said that maybe the reason we couldn't find the chip was because Ronnie got to it first, and he used it to build his own homework machine. I didn't believe it at the time.

RONNIE TEOTWAWKI. GRADE 6

The more I worked with the superchip, the more I could see how powerful it was. I mean, the thing wasn't just *fast*, it could *think* like a person. It had artificial intelligence. If somebody wanted to, they could use it to hack into government databases. They could steal Social Security numbers or credit card numbers. Transfer money without people knowing it. It could bring down the Internet. Not that I would ever do any of that stuff, of course. But I could if I wanted to.

Homework? Who cared about homework? That was the least of it. I could use the chip to do just about anything I wanted and nobody would ever know. I figured it was gonna be a great new year.

KELSEY DONNELLY. GRADE 6

We had a little Christmas party in our class. Mr. Murphy was telling stories about his years in the space program. At some point, Brenton and Snik went off in the corner, whispering to each other. It wasn't like Snik. He's usually the life of the party, cracking jokes and everything. Judy and I went over to see what was up. Snik just looked at us and said, "We think Ronnie found the little red light." And Brenton said, "We've got to get it back."

Chapter 5

January

BRENTON DAMAGATCHI, GRADE 6

Over the holidays, I almost stopped checking my e-mail. I dreaded hearing from Milner again. The only good thing, I remember telling myself, was that if Milner kept bothering me, he didn't know where the chip was. If Ronnie had the chip and he teamed up with Milner, there was no telling what they might do with it.

JUDY DOUGLAS, GRADE 6

When we returned from vacation, Mr. Murphy asked us to write about our favorite gift we got or gave. Mine was a piano! We got it for the whole family. It was used, but it sounds great. I'm going to take piano lessons soon.

KELSEY DONNELLY. GRADE 6

I got a worm composting bin. It is real cool. They give you a pound of red earthworms with it. Then you just throw your food scraps in and the worms eat it and turn it into rich organic compost that you can use in your garden or with your plants. So there's less garbage going into landfills and you become a part of the circle of life.

SAM DAWKINS. GRADE 6

I got this rocket called "Eggscaliber." This is the coolest rocket ever. You can actually mount an egg on the nose cone and shoot it 610 feet up in the air! I really don't know why anybody would want to shoot an egg 610 feet in the air. But it is cool. They call the egg an "eggstronaut."

BRENTON DAMAGATCHI. GRADE 6

We don't exchange gifts in our family. It should not be necessary to give someone a material object to show that you care for them.

RONNIE TEOTWAWKI. GRADE 6

I got a handheld GPS. You know, one of those global positioning systems? It's sort of like the navigation systems you see in cars, but this one is for hikers. Mine is about the size of a walkie-talkie, and it is amazing. It can pinpoint your exact location anywhere on earth, give or take twenty feet. You can't get lost. You see yourself as a little blip like on a radar screen and you can zoom in on any part of the country. It also works as a barometric altimeter, an electronic compass, and you can download topo maps. It's waterproof, too. The thing is amazing.

MR. MURPHY, SIXTH-GRADE TEACHER

Over the holidays, I finally had some time to sit down and read over that old *Phoenix Gazette* article Judy showed me back in November. Apparently, the Smithsonian Institute sent a man named G. E. Kinkaid to explore the Grand Canyon in 1908. He reported that he discovered a mile-long cavern far below the rim. It had tunnels radiating out like the spokes of a wheel, with hundreds of rooms inside.

The article went on to say that Kinkaid found all kinds of artifacts in those tunnels. Swords. Copper tools. Tiny carved heads. Water vessels made from gold. Cave paintings of animals drawn with charcoal. He found a large statue, an idol, sitting cross-legged, with a flower in each hand. The face was Asian. Like a Buddha. These people obviously reached a high stage of civilization.

And here's the most interesting part. Along with all that other stuff, G. E. Kinkaid found a crypt with mummies, and it was surrounded by stone tablets with what looked like Egyptian hieroglyphics written on them.

So my natural question was, what the heck were ancient Egyptians doing in the Grand Canyon long before Columbus? How did they get there? And what happened to all that stuff that was found? Where is it today? Who's got it? Where can I go to see it?

I'll tell you, this article really got my juices flowing. It was hard to sleep that night knowing I was just a few miles away from what could be the most important archeological discovery in American history. I got up and looked through all my American history books. There wasn't a single word about any treasures hidden inside the Grand Canyon. Where were they?

SAM DAWKINS. GRADE 6

Brenton and I decided that Ronnie couldn't be

trusted with that computer chip. We had to get it back. Who knew what he might be capable of doing with it? One of us was going to have to break into his house and take it. There was no other way.

JUDY DOUGLAS. GRADE 6

I want it on the record that I was completely against the idea of breaking into Ronnie's house to steal the chip. There were so many reasons. . . .

1. We would probably get caught.
2. We would get into serious trouble.
3. We could get killed. What if Ronnie's mom had a gun or a vicious guard dog or something?
4. It would be on our permanent records. The other kids don't think about this stuff, but if you break the law, it ends up in some database somewhere. It will follow you for the rest of your life. It might prevent you from getting into law school, or getting a job twenty years from now. Why risk it?
5. It was simply wrong! You don't go breaking into other people's houses.

KELSEY DONNELLY. GRADE 6

We can't get in trouble if we're honest here, right? Well, then, I must admit, I thought the idea of breaking into Ronnie's house and stealing the chip sounded exciting. Nothing exciting ever happens around here.

BRENTON DAMAGATCHI. GRADE 6

Judy has a very black-and-white view of the world, and I don't mean race. To her, everything is either right or wrong, good or bad. But sometimes there's a gray area. In certain situations, breaking the law is the morally correct thing to do. Like, if the American colonists had not rebelled against the British and overthrown their government, there would be no United States today.

With that chip, Ronnie was capable of doing just about anything. So breaking into his house to take the chip and prevent him from using it for criminal activities was the morally correct thing to do. I thought so, anyway.

SAM DAWKINS. GRADE 6

We were having a tough time convincing Judy that breaking into Ronnie Teotwawki's house was the right thing to do. Brenton was doodling on a pad of paper, and suddenly he says, "You know, I always thought Teotwawki was a Japanese name. But it's not. I think I just figured out what it means."

KELSEY DONNELLY. GRADE 6

We all gathered around to look at Brenton's pad. He held it up, and this is what it said:

The
End
Of
The
World
As
We
Know
It

JUDY DOUGLAS. GRADE 6

I said, "We must get that chip."

MR. MURPHY. SIXTH-GRADE TEACHER

After reading that article, I started becoming obsessed with the treasures of the Grand Canyon. The *Phoenix Gazette* never ran a follow-up article about that explorer Kinkaid. I couldn't find a word about him anywhere else. What happened to him? How could a story that big end there?

At first I thought that maybe it was just a newspaper hoax. But they ran it on the front page! Kinkaid was hired by the Smithsonian Institute! And the story was so long and detailed. It didn't seem likely that somebody would have just made it up.

It occurred to me that maybe somebody didn't want the general public to know about this discovery. I mean, when I was a kid they taught us that North America was settled by ice age explorers who came across the Bering Strait from Asia. They became the native Americans. Nobody crossed the Atlantic or Pacific Oceans to get here in ancient times. That's what all the scientists believed. That's what they told us in school.

But what if that was all wrong? What if the ancient Egyptians found a way to get here and they settled in the Grand Canyon? Maybe the scientific community would rather not admit they had it all wrong. Maybe it was a big cover-up.

I started thinking that I should go see if I could find the location of the caverns myself.

KELSEY DONNELLY. GRADE 6

We played "Rock Paper Scissors" to decide which one of us would break into Ronnie's house to steal the chip. Judy lost. So naturally, she started in whining and saying she couldn't do it. Hey, I didn't blame her. I wouldn't have been able to do it either. In the end, we all agreed that Snik was the only one who had the nerve to break into somebody's house. But the three of us agreed beforehand that if he got caught, we would all say we were in on it. It wouldn't be fair for Snik to take the blame.

SAM DAWKINS. GRADE 6

Ronnie's parents work during the day, and I knew that Ronnie belongs to some geeky computer club that meets after school on Wednesdays. So that seemed like a good time.

We all rode over to Ronnie's and parked our bikes a block away. I snuck over to the house and rang the bell. Nobody answered. I tested the doors. They were all locked, but there was a window in the back that opened.

The only problem was, the instant I lifted it up, all these bells started ringing and a dog started barking. I slammed the window down and ran out of there. I didn't stop running until I was on my bike and heading home. I don't think anybody saw us.

RONNIE TEOTWAWKI. GRADE 6

As soon as I put the chip inside my computer, it was obvious that it was super powerful. You know how cell phones have a clock in them, and they're always right, even if you change time zones? Well, for the heck of it, I used my computer to change the time to one minute later. Then I changed it right back. If I wanted to, I could change the time on every cell phone in America. That was how powerful this thing was. I mean, it wasn't just super fast at crunching numbers. It could *think*. If you told it to do something and it couldn't do it, the chip would try something *else*. It was like a human brain doing problem-solving. It could learn. The possibilities were unlimited.

SAM DAWKINS. GRADE 6

I had no choice. We had to get that computer chip back from Ronnie. I walked up to him after school one day and just demanded that he give it to me. I told him I would beat him up unless he gave it to me. It was all bluff, you know? I wasn't about to fight Ronnie. But I didn't know what else to do.

RONNIE TEOTWAWKI. GRADE 6

I figured it was probably Snik who set off the alarm at my house. When he told me he wanted the chip back, I pretended like I didn't know what he was talking about. To tell you the truth, I thought those guys had a lot of nerve, chucking their homework machine into the Grand Canyon and expecting me to just hand the chip over to them. If they wanted it so badly, they shouldn't have thrown it away in the first place. That's what I should have told him. When Snik threatened to beat me up, I told him to lay off or I'd call the cops and tell them that he was trying to break into my house. That shut him up.

BRENTON DAMAGATCHI. GRADE 6

After New Year's, I never heard from Milner again. I figured he lost interest, or he decided to bother somebody else. Anyway, I was relieved.

JUDY DOUGLAS. GRADE 6

After New Year's, Mr. Murphy changed. Everybody noticed it. It seemed like he wasn't that interested in teaching anymore. He would show us videos half the time instead of doing a lesson. He seemed distracted.

MR. MURPHY. SIXTH-GRADE TEACHER

The Hopi Indians, I learned, tell their children that their ancestors once lived in an underground world inside the Grand Canyon. At some point they decided to leave, but there was no way out. Their chief caused a tree to grow, and the people climbed out. They sent a message of thanks to the Temple of the Sun, but that messenger never returned. And today, in Hopi villages at sun-down, the old men of the tribe gaze toward the sun, looking for the messenger. They believe that when he returns, their ancient dwelling place will be returned to them.

RONNIE TEOTWAWKI. GRADE 6

A couple of days after our burglar alarm went off, my cell phone rings and a guy says his name is Richard Milner and he wanted to talk to me. Never heard of him. I figured he was some perv, or maybe *he* was really the one who tried to break into our house. How he got my number, I'll never know.

Anyway, this Milner guy says he wants to meet me, and that it had something to do with a computer chip. I asked him how he knew I had the chip, and he told me he intercepted an e-mail from Brenton to Snik. He knew all about the homework machine, and that they threw it into the Grand Canyon.

So I arranged to meet him at the Canyon View Information Plaza. I figured I could call the cops on my cell phone if there was a problem.

Well, I think we spent an hour talking. We hit it off right away. He told me that he started out as a marketing guy who made his living by figuring out what junk teenagers want to buy—DVDs, video games, fashions, software, and other stuff. But gradually, he learned that with the power of the computer, he can control people's minds and make them do just about *anything* for fun and profit.

He said he needed a smart kid who knew his way around computers. Brenton turned him down, so he thought I could help him with the tech stuff. He would be the idea man.

I liked the guy. I liked the way he operated.

We decided to team up and split whatever we earned fifty-fifty. Shook hands on it.

The first thing we agreed on was that it would be great to have another chip just like the first one. That would double the power and let us link up two computers in a network. Man, we could control the world if we wanted to!

RICHARD MILNER. PERSONAL DIARY

1/22: Met with Ronnie Teotwawki. Need him to get at chip and kids. Agreed to work as a team. Booked flight to Tokyo to buy another chip.

MR. MURPHY. SIXTH-GRADE TEACHER

I rented a kayak one weekend and did a little poking around the Grand Canyon, looking for the site of the ancient caverns.

The canyon is enormous, of course. Two hundred seventy-seven miles along the Colorado River. All I had was the information in the *Phoenix Gazette* article, and a hiker's map. I didn't even bring binoculars. I only had a general idea of where to look. I didn't find anything.

KELSEY DONNELLY. GRADE 6

Mr. Murphy gave us an assignment to write a one-page essay on what we did over the weekend. I wrote a letter to my congressman saying we should put solar panels on every roof in Arizona to generate electricity so we won't have to burn fossil fuels anymore. Then I wrote an essay about how I wrote a letter to my congressman saying we should put solar panels on every roof in Arizona to generate electricity so we won't have to burn fossil fuels anymore.

MR. MURPHY. SIXTH-GRADE TEACHER

I was collecting their essays when Sam Dawkins raised his hand and asked me what I did over the weekend. So I told the kids I went kayaking in the canyon and I told them about the article in the *Phoenix Gazette*. Judy knew about it, of course, because she was the one who found it in the first place. But she had just read the first few paragraphs. She didn't know all the details.

I'll tell you one thing I noticed. When I was describing the caverns and treasures, the mummies and everything, everybody was fascinated.

But the one who tuned in the most was Ronnie Teotwawki. It was the first time I ever saw that boy pay attention in class. He was staring at me, and he was hanging on every word.

Chapter 6

February

RONNIE TEOTWAWKI. GRADE 6

I'm not really a book guy. I figure that if the stuff in libraries was so great, they wouldn't have to give it away for free. You know what I mean? But when Mr. Murphy told us there was an ancient Egyptian treasure hidden in a cave in the Grand Canyon, I went straight to the library after school. I had to look at that article he was telling us about.

It wasn't hard to find. The library keeps old issues of the *Phoenix Gazette*. There it was, right on the front page. April 5, 1909. It said there were golden statues, weapons, mummies, and all kinds of other stuff hidden in a cave right here in the Grand Canyon. This explorer guy named Kinkaid supposedly found all this stuff. But nobody knows what happened to it. It's not in any museum. There's no record of Kinkaid taking the stuff out of the canyon. Either it vanished . . . or maybe it was still there. There was no record of what happened to Kinkaid either.

Man, I sat there and felt the hair on my neck rising up. If this article was for real, and the stuff was still sitting there a century later, what was to stop *me* from getting it? Nothing. Finders keepers. Maybe I could use the GPS I got for Christmas to help me find it.

The article was real long. There was a lot of detail about the location of the cave. I made a photocopy of the article so I could go over it real carefully.

SAM DAWKINS. GRADE 6

Everybody was buzzing after Mr. Murphy told us about this treasure hidden in the Grand Canyon. I met up with Brenton in the playground after school and told him that I was gonna try to find it. He said he would help.

Kelsey and Judy came over and asked what we were whispering about. When I told them, they laughed and said we were silly. But when we told them we were serious, they said they wanted in on it too. We all agreed that if we found any treasure, we would donate it to a museum.

JUDY DOUGLAS. GRADE 6

The four of us went to the library after school so we could read the *Phoenix Gazette* article carefully. And guess who was sitting there in the periodicals room? Ronnie Teotwawki! I could hardly believe my eyes. He probably never set foot in a library in his life!

RONNIE TEOTWAWKI. GRADE 6

The four of them walked into the library and saw me sitting there. Judy was all, "What are *you* doing here?" Like I'm not allowed in the library, right? I told her it's a public place and I have as much right to be there as she does.

KELSEY DONNELLY. GRADE 6

Ronnie left the library after we came in, but we saw his name on the sheet of paper you have to sign if you want to look at the old newspapers on microfilm. We knew exactly what Ronnie was doing there. He wanted to find out the location of the treasure. Just like us.

JUDY DOUGLAS. GRADE 6

We copied the article and I asked the librarian if we could look at some maps of the Grand Canyon. She had a whole bunch of them, some recent ones and some dating back to the 1920s when they were still exploring it. Mr. Murphy wasn't very specific about where the treasure was. Maybe he didn't know himself.

Every summer, millions of tourists come here. They usually only go to Grand Canyon Village, where the visitor center is and there are some hotels. But the whole canyon is hundreds of miles along the Colorado River. Even if the secret cavern was as big as Mr. Murphy said it was, locating it would be like finding a needle in a haystack.

BRENTON DAMAGATCHI. GRADE 6

I often wonder if there is a square inch on this planet that has never been stepped on by a human foot. If such a place exists, it would probably be in the Grand Canyon. I've done some hiking in the canyon, and it is just so vast that it would be hard to imagine all of it has been explored. Even today.

SAM DAWKINS. GRADE 6

Brenton unrolled this old map and we were looking it over. Judy got a magnifying glass from the librarian so we could read the tiny print. That's when we noticed something. On the north side of the canyon, in the area around Ninety-Four Mile Creek and Trinity Creek, there were a whole bunch of rock formations with names that sounded Egyptian or Hindu—Tower of Ra, Horus Temple, Osiris Temple, Isis Temple, Cheops Pyramid, the Buddha Cloister, Buddha Temple, Manu Temple, Shiva Temple. Stuff like that. Brenton and I turned to each other and whispered, "That's where it is."

MR. MURPHY. SIXTH-GRADE TEACHER

It didn't occur to me at the time that the kids would get so excited about the idea of a secret treasure in the Grand Canyon. I had come to believe that kids today don't care about stuff like that. They just want to watch TV and go on YouTube. I certainly didn't think they would actually make the effort to try and find a real treasure. It's so much easier to play a video game and find a virtual treasure.

It was around Presidents' Day. I remember, because I told them to do a research project about the presidents. As usual, Brenton turned in the most interesting paper. I even saved it. . . .

HOW TALL WERE THE PRESIDENTS?
by Brenton Damagatchi

Below is a list of the presidents, starting with the tallest (Lincoln) and ending with the shrimpy James Madison. Twenty-four presidents were under six feet tall, and eighteen were six feet tall or more.

Abraham Lincoln	6 ft 4 in
Lyndon B. Johnson	6 ft 3 ½ in
Bill Clinton	
Thomas Jefferson	6 ft 2 ½ in
Chester A. Arthur	
George H. W. Bush	
Franklin D. Roosevelt	
George Washington	6 ft 2 in
Andrew Jackson	
Ronald Reagan	6 ft 1 in
James Buchanan	
Gerald Ford	

James Garfield

Warren Harding

John F. Kennedy

James Monroe

William Howard Taft

John Tyler	6 ft 0 in
Richard Nixon	5 ft 11 ½ in
George W. Bush	
Grover Cleveland	
Herbert Hoover	
Woodrow Wilson	5 ft 11 in
Dwight D. Eisenhower	5 ft 10 ½ in
Calvin Coolidge	
Andrew Johnson	
Franklin Pierce	
Theodore Roosevelt	5 ft 10 in
Jimmy Carter	
Millard Fillmore	
Harry S. Truman	5 ft 9 in
Rutherford B. Hayes	5 ft 8 ½ in
William Henry Harrison	
James Polk	
Zachary Taylor	
Ulysses S. Grant	5 ft 7 ¾ in
John Adams	

John Quincy Adams	
William McKinley	5 ft 7 in
Benjamin Harrison	
Martin Van Buren	5 ft 6 in
James Madison	5 ft 3 ¾ in

RONNIE TEOTWAWKI. GRADE 6

I was wondering what was taking Milner so long to get back with the second superchip. It was around the end of February when he finally called me on my cell. He was home from Japan. I asked him if he was able to get another superchip, but he shushed me and said we couldn't talk about stuff like that over the phone because somebody might be listening in. I agreed to meet him at the Canyon View Information Plaza.

I don't know what the big deal was, because when we met up, all he had to say was that he *didn't* get another superchip. It wasn't because it was too expensive. It just didn't exist. The one we had was a prototype. We had the only one in the world. And in fact, he told me he was worried that some Japanese gangsters might have followed him home, because they wanted the first superchip back. I remember thinking, *This guy is paranoid.*

Anyway, without a second superchip, we wouldn't be able to link up two computers in a network and do all kinds of cool stuff with it. It was a good idea, anyway.

We got to talking about stuff, and I happened to mention that newspaper article and the treasure of the Grand Canyon. I had the Xerox I made at the library with me, and I showed it to Milner. Well, his eyes lit up like headlights! It was like he forgot about the superchip and all he wanted to talk about was hiking into the canyon for the treasure. He kept saying, "I've got to find it. I've got to find it."

I was a little P.O.'d, you know? I mean, he didn't know anything about the treasure until I told him about it. If anybody should get it, it should be me. I got him to agree to work as a team. It made sense for me, because he was a grown-up and he'd be able to get us a raft and supplies and all the stuff we'd need to go after the treasure.

POLICE CHIEF REBECCA FISH

Startin' 'round the end of February, every coupla days a few more people would show up at the south entrance gate. They came in buses, cars, some of 'em hitchhiked. A lot of 'em used frequent-flyer miles. One guy claimed he walked from Alabama. They came from all over. Some of 'em were runaways. They weren't your usual tourists who want to see the canyon with their own eyes, snap some pictures, buy some souvenirs, and get on home.

No, they all said the same thing—the end of the world is comin' on Mother's Day. Claimed the canyon is gonna open up and the earth'll cleave in half, like a busted Wiffle ball. They'll be saved. I have no idea where they got them crazy ideas. What a bunch of nuts! Must've been the Twinkies they were all eating. They called themselves "Canyonists." Put 'em on a bus and sent 'em home. Or we tried to, anyhow. After a while there were too many of 'em to round up.

You'd see these raggedy people wanderin' around, lookin' for food in garbage cans and so forth. I'll tell you, they were worse than the bears! They would all be babblin' about aliens and some prophet named Notnerb. Sometimes you'd see a group of 'em out in the middle of a field, standin' on their heads in a circle. Strangest thing.

The Grand Canyon is a place for folks who

wanna appreciate the beauty of nature. This ain't no place for weirdos.

JUDY DOUGLAS. GRADE 6

Snik and Kelsey wanted to rush off and go look for the treasure—that afternoon! They were just going to hike down and get it. It was as if they were going to the store to get a loaf of bread. That's the way they do things. Act now and think things through later.

So I said to them, do you realize we're seven thousand feet above sea level? Do you realize it takes a full day to hike down to the river and another full day to hike back up? Where are we going to get a raft? How are we going to pay for it? And what if there *is* some fabulous treasure down there? How are we going to carry it back out? You can't just go running off to do crazy stuff. You've got to plan things.

MR. MURPHY. SIXTH-GRADE TEACHER

Judy, Brenton, Sam, and Kelsey came to me one day after school and said they wanted to talk in private. I figured it was about schoolwork, but it wasn't. They told me they wanted to hike down into the canyon and search for the secret cave that was mentioned in that newspaper article. They asked for my help.

Well, I must admit that I was flattered, honored, and pleased that they were interested. So many of the kids here never even venture below the rim of the canyon. This could be the ultimate field trip. A real teachable moment. It was extremely doubtful that there was any treasure to be found, but they would learn about indigenous plants, trees, insects, wildlife, and the geology of the canyon.

I'd be lying if I didn't admit that I wanted to give it another shot at finding the secret caverns myself. These kids were young and strong, and they would be a lot of help.

On the other hand, it could be dangerous. Accidents happen. I wasn't sure I wanted to be responsible for the safety of four kids. I thought it over and agreed to be their chaperone if they each got their parents to sign a permission form.

February is a bit too cold to be taking long hikes in the canyon. The summer is too hot. It gets up over a hundred degrees, and people have been known to die out there from heat exhaustion.

I thought a weekend in April or May would be perfect.

RONNIE TEOTWAWKI. GRADE 6

I'm not sure if it was me or Milner who came up with the idea. Probably me. I was fooling around with the GPS I got for Christmas. It was pretty cool, but the capabilities were limited. That's when I started to wonder what would happen if I took the superchip out of my computer and put it in my handheld GPS instead. It would make it into a super GPS!

And a super GPS was just the thing I needed, because it could lead me right to the location of the secret caverns. Right to the treasure of the Grand Canyon.

Chapter 7

March

MR. MURPHY. SIXTH-GRADE TEACHER

One of the things we spend a lot of time on in sixth grade is ancient Egypt. They were a fascinating people, and the kids were fascinated by them. I got some videos from the library to show them what life was like in the time of the pharaohs.

BRENTON DAMAGATCHI. GRADE 6

What interested me the most were the pyramids. Six million tons of stone. Some of the blocks weigh nine tons. Think about it. The wheel wasn't invented yet. The only tools the Egyptians had to move and carry all that stone were wood and rope. So how did they build the pyramids? I'll tell you how. They didn't. Aliens had to have built them. Did you know that the Great Pyramid is lined up exactly with the magnetic north pole of the Earth? That can't be coincidence. The compass hadn't been invented yet either.

If you go on the Internet, there's a lot of evidence that people couldn't have built the pyramids. It had to be aliens.

SAM DAWKINS. GRADE 6

The coolest thing about the Egyptians was the way they preserved their dead guys. They would pull their organs out and make them into mummies. They would break their nose, and then bust the brain into little pieces so they could pull it out through where the nose used to be. I'm not making this stuff up. And then, get this, they would fill the skull with sawdust! Sounds like some people I know, and they're still alive.

Mr. Murphy told us he went to a museum in Egypt once and they had a special mummy room. You had to pay a separate admission just to see the mummies. So he paid the admission and went in. And you know how when you see mummies in cartoons they're all wrapped

tape and stuff? Well, these mummies
unwrapped. Mr. Murphy said it was like
king at meat in a supermarket. Gross! But
mummies are cool. The Egyptians mummified
cats and crocodiles too. They really loved their
mummies.

KELSEY DONNELLY. GRADE 6

The ancient Egyptians worshipped Ra the
sun god, Horus the sky god, and Osiris the god
of the dead. They believed that every day, Ra
sailed across the sky in a boat. And then at night
he would disappear into the underworld of the
west. There was another Nile River there, they
believed. Osiris pulled the boat along this river
until morning, when the sun rose again. It was
actually very beautiful.

JUDY DOUGLAS. GRADE 6

I liked that the ancient Egyptians were a
peaceful people. They created beautiful art,
architecture, sculpture, and writing. Mr.
Murphy told us that for years and years, nobody
was able to translate Egyptian hieroglyphics.
Then they found this thing called the Rosetta

Stone, which was a tablet that had a passage written in three different languages. After many years they finally translated them, and they were able to figure out what the hieroglyphics meant.

MR. MURPHY, SIXTH-GRADE TEACHER
Everything about ancient Egypt interested the kids. But what really made their eyes bug out was when we got to King Tutankhamen. I guess it was because Tut was nine years old when he became pharaoh, and he was only nineteen when he died. Kids can relate to that.

JUDY DOUGLAS, GRADE 6
Mr. Murphy told us that a British archeologist named Howard Carter searched for the tomb of King Tut for fifteen years until he finally found it in the Valley of the Kings in 1922. He reached a sealed doorway to a burial chamber. When he opened it and peered inside with a candle, there was King Tut's tomb, completely intact. It was made of solid gold, and it was surrounded by lots of other golden things, jewels, treasures, and all the boy king's possessions.

KELSEY DONNELLY. GRADE 6

King Tut's tomb had a curse, you know. They all did. There were warnings around the body: "Death shall come on swift wings to him that touches the tomb of the Pharaoh." I think it was true. Most people don't know that the guy who hired Howard Carter to find King Tut died five months after they opened the tomb. He was bitten by a mosquito and it got infected. I looked it up.

SAM DAWKINS. GRADE 6

Kelsey tried to scare us with all that curse baloney. She said that if we found the secret treasure of the Grand Canyon, there might be a curse on it. I wasn't buying that mumbo jumbo. Of course she would fall for that curse stuff. She'll fall for anything. I couldn't wait to leave for our trip.

MR. MURPHY. SIXTH-GRADE TEACHER

It was astonishing to me that most of these kids have lived within a mile of the Grand Canyon their whole lives, but none of them had ever hiked all the way down to the Colorado River. When I asked them why not, they just shrugged and said they never thought about it. Amazing!

Hiking a mile down into the canyon is not like a stroll in the woods. I spent the next few weeks after school preparing for our trip. Being responsible for the safety of four kids, I wanted to make sure nothing went wrong. I got a wilderness permit so we could legally stay overnight in the backcountry. There were maps we would need, and lots of gear.

SAM DAWKINS. GRADE 6

I couldn't believe how much junk we had to lug with us for just a long weekend. Flashlights, headlamps, extra batteries, a first-aid kit, walking sticks, Swiss Army knives, cameras, sleeping bags, garbage bags. We had to bring signal mirrors in case we got into trouble and had to get help. Mr. Murphy told us that cell phones usually don't work at the bottom of the canyon.

JUDY DOUGLAS. GRADE 6

. . . suntan lotion, lip balm, polarizing sunglasses, wide-brimmed hats to keep the sun off our faces. Mr. Murphy told us each to bring a handkerchief so we could soak it in the river and cool off.

KELSEY DONNELLY. GRADE 6

. . . high-sodium snacks like nuts, pretzels, beef jerky, energy bars. Water. Lots of water. They say that if you hike down into the canyon in the summertime, you need to drink a gallon of water a day.

SAM DAWKINS. GRADE 6

And, of course, you have to bring your own toilet paper, and a metal shovel . . . for burying your own waste!

JUDY DOUGLAS. GRADE 6

Ugh! Disgusting!

RONNIE TEOTWAWKI. GRADE 6

Milner and I met at the visitor center one day after school. I opened up my GPS and took out the chip that was in there. I carefully replaced it with the superchip and turned it on. Neither of us was expecting it to work.

Well, I plugged in some information from the *Phoenix Gazette* article and the GPS started humming. It felt alive in my hand. Like, magnetic, you know? It was like one of those divining rods that finds water. No, it was more like a dog that's so anxious to go for a walk that it pulls you to the door.

JUDY DOUGLAS. GRADE 6

We have spring break the second week in April. So there's no school for a few days and the weather is usually perfect. It would be a good time to go.

RICHARD MILNER. PERSONAL DIARY

March 27: Met with Ronnie. Agreed to search for treasure on or around April 15, when he is off from school.

KELSEY DONNELLY. GRADE 6

I know it's easy to say now, but from the beginning I really felt the trip was a mistake. I didn't tell anybody at the time. But I just had an intuition that something was going to go wrong. Finding a treasure didn't mean anything to me. Who cares about that stuff? I was filled with a sense of foreboding.

Chapter 8

April

SAM DAWKINS, GRADE 6

You need to know *all* the details of what happened that weekend? Okay. It's a long story. Where do I start?

I remember we had to get up super early because Mr. Murphy said it wasn't safe to be hiking in the middle of the day when the sun is high in the sky. So we all met at the Bright Angel Lodge at six a.m. That wasn't fun. I like to sleep late when I'm on vacation.

I'd hiked below the rim before, of course. But not very far. I'd usually go an hour or so and come back up. I'd never been all the way down to the river. That's a *long* hike.

They've got these signs all over the trail warning you to turn back if you're not in good shape, if you have a heart condition, if you didn't bring enough water, stuff like that. They say that nobody should try to hike all the way down to the river and back in one day. There's this one sign that always cracks me up—it's a stick figure of a hiker down on his hands and knees, and he's puking his guts out. Hey, if you get in trouble, you can't say nobody warned you.

MR. MURPHY, SIXTH-GRADE TEACHER

There are a number of trails that lead from the South Rim of the canyon down to the Colorado River. I chose the Bright Angel Trail because it's the easiest and most gradual. These kids were not experienced hikers, and I didn't want anyone to get hurt. Even so, it's almost eight miles to the river with all the switchbacks, a 4,380-foot descent.

KELSEY DONNELLY, GRADE 6

I didn't tell the others, but I had never hiked in my life. I'm sure they'd make fun of me. It's a little embarrassing. I grew up less than a mile from the Grand Canyon, but I never even set foot below the rim until that day we went looking for the blinking red light.

It was scary when we started out. I'm not afraid of heights or anything, but as soon as we went below the rim, it looks like you're about to drop off a cliff. If you took a couple of steps in the wrong direction, you could fall off a rock and die.

JUDY DOUGLAS. GRADE 6

Everybody was in good spirits when we started out. Snik was cracking jokes and making fun of everybody. The trail is smooth and wide. It's easy walking downhill, of course. Climbing back up is a lot harder. They say it takes twice as long to hike out as it does to hike in. We were anxious to get down to the river, but we went slowly. Mr. Murphy said we had to take a ten-minute break every hour. Even if we weren't tired.

KELSEY DONNELLY. GRADE 6

It was dirty and dusty. They actually let mules carry people and supplies on the trail. Mules! We all had to move aside to let a bunch of mules go by. So I had another thing to worry about—stepping in mule manure. I really don't like hiking.

MR. MURPHY. SIXTH-GRADE TEACHER

A lot of chipmunks and squirrels were scampering around. I hoped that the kids might get the chance to see some bobcats, mountain lions, and bighorn sheep too. There are actually something like fifteen hundred plant and four hundred animal species living in the Grand Canyon today. Some of them have been here since the Ice Age.

SAM DAWKINS. GRADE 6

Mr. Murphy was being all teacherlike. He'd say, "Look, kids, there's a whiptail lizard!" and tell us some random fact about it. Or, "Ooh, check out that peregrine falcon! He can fly two hundred and fifty miles an hour!" I think that in teacher school they must tell all the teachers in training that they have to always be teaching, whether or not there's anything worth learning. I was making fun of him, but in a nice way. He's a good guy.

BRENTON DAMAGATCHI. GRADE 6

We came upon a little carving on the wall. It was a stick figure of a person running. Everybody thought it was graffiti, but Mr. Murphy told us it was a pictograph, sort of a prehistoric doodle. Some ancient cartoonist was trying to talk to us, but we didn't know what he was saying. Snik wanted to make a rubbing of it, but Mr. Murphy told him not to because that would damage it. You're not even supposed to touch them. We took some pictures instead. You know what they say—take only pictures, leave only footprints.

My mom once told me that when she was young, they taught kids in school that Columbus "discovered" America. They made a big deal about celebrating Columbus Day. Then they found out that people lived in America more than three thousand years before Columbus was even born. Oops! That must have been embarrassing.

JUDY DOUGLAS. GRADE 6

We took a break at the Mile-and-a-Half Resthouse. Funny name. It's nothing fancy, but they have toilets, picnic tables, and an emergency telephone. We could get out of the sun for a while. It was already getting hot. Mr. Murphy kept telling us we should eat before we get hungry and drink before we get thirsty. He said plenty of hikers get heat exhaustion.

SAM DAWKINS. GRADE 6

Mr. Murphy told us that over seven hundred people have died at the Grand Canyon. Seven hundred! It happens all the time. People get struck by lightning, or they drown in the rapids of the Colorado River. There are flash floods, snake bites, rock falls. And of course, lots of people run out of water, become dehydrated, and drop dead.

People can be just dumb, too. In 1993, he told us, these two guys from California jumped into the canyon with parachutes. Their chutes opened, but they got tangled on the way down, and that was it for them.

KELSEY DONNELLY. GRADE 6

Mr. Murphy said that lots of guys think it's fun to pee off really high places. Like a cliff. Judy and I thought that was totally repulsive, but the boys said it sounded cool. The only problem is that some of these guys lose their balance while they're peeing and fall into the canyon. Boys can be so stupid. I started looking up to make sure nobody was going to pee on us . . . or fall on us.

JUDY DOUGLAS. GRADE 6

Mr. Murphy told us that a lot of people even died while they were just posing for pictures. Can you imagine? Somebody would be taking a picture of their friend or something, and they'd say back up a little to get a good view, and their friend would back up and fall off a cliff. Snik laughed; I told him that it wasn't funny. What a horrible way to die. You shouldn't laugh at other people's misfortunes.

MR. MURPHY. SIXTH-GRADE TEACHER

I probably shouldn't have told them about the tragedies at the Grand Canyon, but it did help pass the time while we were hiking. I didn't tell them about the people who came to the canyon to commit suicide. Or the nuts who drove their cars over the edge on purpose. Or the murders that took place there.

In 1956, a plane was flying from Los Angeles to Kansas City with seventy people onboard. Another plane was flying in the same direction toward Chicago with fifty-eight people. The two pilots decided it would be interesting to fly over the Grand Canyon to give the passengers a view. The only problem was that they crashed into each other, and everybody died. It was one of the worst air tragedies ever at the time. I didn't want to scare the kids.

KELSEY DONNELLY. GRADE 6

There was another rest house at the three-mile mark. My legs were already hurting from walking downhill. Mr. Murphy was making fun of us. He said we were out of shape because we spend too much time watching TV and surfing the Internet.

I took my boots off and he told me to be careful when I put them back on. When I asked him why, he said a scorpion might have crawled into them. Great! Now I had to worry about stepping in mule manure, guys peeing on my head or falling off cliffs, and scorpions crawling into my boots. I was ready to go home.

SAM DAWKINS. GRADE 6

I picked up a nice walking stick. I wanted to kill a snake with it. You can spot a rattlesnake because they have a diamond-shaped pattern on their back. They usually hide from the sun, so they're hard to find. Unless, of course, you sit in some shady spot where one of them decides to take a nap. Mr. Murphy told us that if we saw a rattler we should just leave it alone and it would leave us alone. But I wanted to kill one. It would make a good souvenir.

BRENTON DAMAGATCHI. GRADE 6

As you wend your way down the switch-backs on the trail, you can see the texture and the colors change on the sides of the canyon. It goes from cream to pinkish white. So you're actually walking from one geological time period into the previous one. It occurred to me that hiking down the canyon is about the closest any of us will ever come to traveling through time. It took millions of years for the river to slice its way through that rock, but we walked past it in a few hours. Even though it seemed like we had been hiking a long time, it sort of put things into perspective.

JUDY DOUGLAS. GRADE 6

We started to see more vegetation—bushes and trees. Some of them had grapes. I was afraid they might be poisonous, but Mr. Murphy said they were okay to eat. I tried one, but it was really tart so I spit it out.

KELSEY DONNELLY. GRADE 6

We came to the Indian Garden Campground. They have a ranger station there, and drinking water. The ranger told us that a long time ago, the Havasupai Indians lived there, and even did farming. He said we had walked almost five miles from the rim. It felt like a hundred. Mr. Murphy only let us rest for a few minutes before we had to gather up our stuff and keep going.

BRENTON DAMAGATCHI. GRADE 6

What struck me was how peaceful it becomes as you get closer to the bottom of the canyon. All the noises you hear in the real world—planes, cars honking, the hum of electrical appliances, people talking too loudly into their cell phones— are gone. It was like I never heard real quiet before. Just the rustling of the wind. The only people who make it this far are the serious hikers. Most tourists only hike a few miles and go back up to the rim. Back up to the real world.

KELSEY DONNELLY. GRADE 6

I've seen all these pictures of the Grand Canyon. But as beautiful as the pictures are, it's not the same as seeing it with your own eyes.

Looking up at the sandstone cliffs just blew me away. I had never seen anything so spectacular. It made me want to protect the environment of this wonderful planet even more.

SAM DAWKINS. GRADE 6

After we left the Indian Garden Campground, we could see the Colorado River plainly and everybody got excited. We were almost there. We passed through some switchbacks called the Devil's Corkscrew, and then there was a steep drop down to Pipe Creek. There was a waterfall near there, and the River Resthouse. I wanted to jump in the water. But there was no time.

KELSEY DONNELLY. GRADE 6

Two more miles and we finally reached the Silver Suspension Bridge. On the other side of the bridge is the Bright Angel Campground, and that's where we camped out for the night. We were all exhausted.

JUDY DOUGLAS. GRADE 6

We rested up and ate dinner. Mr. Murphy had some freeze-dried chicken. It sounded nauseating.

I remember being really hungry and it tasted so good. Food always tastes good after you've been exercising.

By the time we finished eating, it was dark out. It's really cold at the bottom of the canyon, even in April. We all climbed into our sleeping bags to get warm.

BRENTON DAMAGATCHI. GRADE 6

I remember lying there, looking up at the stars, and thinking to myself how lucky I was to be alive. I was in a crack in the earth—one of the Seven Wonders of the World. Most people never get to see the Grand Canyon in their lifetime. And here I was, at the bottom of it.

I could understand why some people would want to believe in Canyonism. I was lying on a rock that could very possibly be two *billion* years old. If you're going to worship something, why *not* the planet that you live on? It's the place that gives you air to breathe, food to eat, water to drink. And after you have those things, what else do you really need? A cell phone? An iPod? Who needs that stuff? I fell asleep almost instantly.

MR. MURPHY. SIXTH-GRADE TEACHER

Most folks who raft the Colorado start out at Lee's Ferry. You usually can't get a raft anywhere near the Bright Angel Campground. But I know a fellow over at Phantom Ranch down there. It's the only commercial tourist facility below the rim. He arranged for us to get an eighteen-foot neoprene raft that could seat the five of us comfortably.

SAM DAWKINS. GRADE 6

Mr. Murphy woke us up and made us put on life jackets before we could get into the raft. That's when it occurred to me—what if we found all those treasures and gold and stuff that we read about in that article? How would we get the stuff back up to the rim? Mr. Murphy said that if there were any treasures, they belonged to the state of Arizona. Bummer!

We all wanted to find the caverns anyway. I wanted to see for myself.

KELSEY DONNELLY. GRADE 6

After we pushed the raft off, the boys were acting all macho, grabbing the paddles and shouting out silly orders. They totally didn't know what they were doing. It was fun to watch. They are so immature.

JUDY DOUGLAS. GRADE 6

The boys were being boys—splashing us with the paddles and so on. Like it was all fun and games. But suddenly, we hit some white water and Snik almost fell out of the raft. That straightened him out quick.

We all had to paddle really hard to avoid the rocks on both sides. The river pulls you along, but you still have to steer. It was fun, but a little scary, too. It was my first time rafting.

SAM DAWKINS. GRADE 6

The water smoothed out as we got close to Ninety-Four Mile Creek and Trinity Creek. This is the area where there are rock formations with Egyptian names—Tower of Ra, Horus Temple, Osiris Temple, Isis Temple, Cheops Pyramid. We put down our paddles and got out binoculars. I started scanning up and down the north side of the canyon. I was looking for an opening in the canyon walls, or maybe a shadow. The secret cavern could have been covered up by trees or bushes. We knew it had to be around there, if it existed at all. With five pairs of eyes, we figured that one of us would see it.

MR. MURPHY. SIXTH-GRADE TEACHER

I had read the *Phoenix Gazette* article very carefully, line by line. But still, I had only a very general idea of where the caverns might be. I knew they had to be pretty well hidden, or some tourist would have stumbled upon them a long time ago. And they were probably pretty high above the river. We'd have to climb up to them if we saw them. Thousands of years ago, when people inhabited caverns, the Grand Canyon wasn't as deep. Maybe it was a short climb up from the river. Now, it would be a longer climb.

Of course I was well aware that the whole story I had read could have simply been an elaborate newspaper hoax. In all probability, there *were* no secret caverns, no hidden treasures. How could ancient Egyptians have found their way to the Grand Canyon in the first place? How could they cross the ocean? It just didn't make sense.

I remember that's what I was thinking, when suddenly our raft bumped into another raft.

SAM DAWKINS, GRADE 6

We were all looking up at the canyon walls through binoculars when our raft crashed into another raft. It was tied to a branch at the north side of the river. Except for the paddles, the only thing on the other raft was a picnic cooler. Everybody freaked out a little, because we hadn't seen another soul on the river since we started out.

I climbed on the other raft and looked for a name or something. That's when I saw the writing on the back of the cooler. It said PROPERTY OF RICHARD MILNER.

Oh, I remembered *that* name. He was the guy who was stalking us when we were using the homework machine. He seemed a little nutty. We put two and two together. Ronnie and Milner must have teamed up. They were looking for the treasure too.

KELSEY DONNELLY, GRADE 6

I couldn't believe it. They beat us there!

We all looked up, thinking we would see them climbing up or down the rocks. But they weren't around.

BRENTON DAMAGATCHI. GRADE 6

I knew right away what happened. Ronnie must have taken our chip from the homework machine and put it into that portable GPS he was always carrying around. That would have been the only way to find the caverns.

KELSEY DONNELLY. GRADE 6

I figured that was it. Let's go home, y'know? But the boys got all excited. They wanted to climb up. Even if we couldn't get any treasure for ourselves, they wanted to see it. So did Mr. Murphy. Judy and I would have been just as happy to call it a day. I wanted to go home and take a good long nap in my own bed.

MR. MURPHY. SIXTH-GRADE TEACHER

I should have stopped it right there. If I'd known then what I know now, I would have ended the trip and gone home. But as they say, hindsight is twenty-twenty.

Milner and I didn't hike down the canyon like the others. We took his van to Lee's Ferry and put the raft in the water there. It was his idea. He said that if we found any treasure, we could load it up in the van and drive it out of there.

The GPS worked like magic. I plugged all the information I had into it, and the thing practically led us straight to the spot where we tied up the raft. You couldn't see any caves from the river and there was no trail, but we had confidence that something was up there. We tied up the raft and started climbing the north wall. It was hard. I remember that I wished I had hiking boots, because my sneakers weren't very good for digging in the cracks in the wall. Luckily there were a lot of vines to grab on to.

We must have climbed nearly two thousand feet up. That's where we started to see stains in the sedimentary formation. Then there was a rock shelf up there, and right above it was the mouth of the cave. The rock shelf hid it from the river.

The opening was about the size of a small doorway, but rounded at the top. There were chisel marks on the wall inside the entrance. It wasn't just a natural cave. People carved it. Those chisel marks were probably thousands of years old. The last time somebody stood on that rock shelf, Columbus hadn't sailed for America yet. I got goose bumps.

Milner and I turned on our flashlights and went inside the cave. There were steps going up, about ten of them. At the top of the steps there was a room, and that's where we found a body. Yeah, a dead body.

SAM DAWKINS. GRADE 6

We tied our raft to the same branch as Milner's raft and started climbing up the rock wall. Yeah, all of us. Even Judy. Even Mr. Murphy. He's in pretty good shape, for an old guy.

JUDY DOUGLAS. GRADE 6

I offered to stay behind and guard the raft. I'm not a rock climber. There were some vines and branches to hold on to, but it looked really scary. Mr. Murphy wanted us all to stay together as group, so I had to climb up. And to be honest, I wanted to see what was up there as much as anybody else.

RONNIE TEOTWAWKI. GRADE 6

I had never seen a dead body before, and I kinda freaked out. I didn't want to touch it. It didn't look like a mummy. It wasn't wrapped or anything, like in the cartoons. It was more like a skeleton, but with clothes on. Regular clothes, not Egyptian clothes. It wasn't ancient or anything.

I felt like I might have to throw up, and I sat down for a minute to catch my breath. Milner wasn't bothered by the body. When he touched it, the skull fell off. He went through the pockets of the clothing until he found a wallet. There were some papers inside it. The name on one sheet was G. E. Kinkaid. I remembered that was the name of the guy in the newspaper article who claimed to have discovered the treasure. And here he was—dead.

JUDY DOUGLAS. GRADE 6

We started climbing up the side of the canyon. I was terrified. Everybody kept saying not to look down, but I couldn't help it. I knew that if I put my foot on a rock and the rock gave way, I would be dead. I would be another one of those idiots Mr. Murphy told us about who fell into the

Grand Canyon. I would become a story that boys like Snik would laugh about someday.

RONNIE TEOTWAWKI. GRADE 6

After G. E. Kinkaid discovered the caverns and told the newspaper about it, he must have gone back to haul out the treasures. Then he died in there. I couldn't tell what happened to him. There weren't any bullet holes or signs that he died violently. I didn't want to investigate too closely though. It grossed me out. For all I knew, he died of starvation in there, all by himself.

Milner told me that if Kinkaid's body was there, the treasures must be there too. He stepped right over the body like it was a pile of laundry.

We shined the flashlights around and there were four or five tunnels going off in different directions. It was like we were at the hub of a bicycle wheel and the tunnels were the spokes. I couldn't tell if they were man-made or not.

MR. MURPHY. SIXTH-GRADE TEACHER

We were very careful climbing up the rock wall. I didn't want any of the kids to get hurt.

For the first time, I entertained the real possibility that we had actually found the secret caverns of the Grand Canyon. The article in the *Phoenix Gazette* may have been factual. The higher we climbed, the more excited I became.

Think about it. For centuries, explorers had been looking for treasure in the Southwest. Back in 1540, a Spaniard named Francisco Vásquez de Coronado led an expedition from Mexico looking for the Seven Cities of Cíbola. There were supposed to be great riches hidden there. He never found anything except the natural beauty of the land. As I climbed up the rock wall, I was excited. Maybe we were going to find what Coronado didn't. We were modern-day explorers.

RONNIE TEOTWAWKI. GRADE 6

Milner and I went into the first tunnel, and it was like when that guy Howard Carter found King Tut's tomb. There was stuff *everywhere*. Big pots made out of clay and straw. Simple wooden chairs. Tools made from some kind of metal. Milner said it must have been the place where food was prepared by whoever lived there. The tunnel went on and on. It was musty.

Instead of exploring the whole thing, we went over to the next tunnel. It was empty, but when we pointed our flashlights at the walls, we could see they were covered with paintings. Mostly they were pictures of animals. Deer and elk. There were some stick figures, too, that looked like people. Some of them were painted, some looked like they were drawn with charcoal, and some were carved right into the wall. It was an ancient art gallery.

Milner said we must be getting close. I remember he said that God would have never built such an incredible underground city unless there was something very special hidden inside it.

SAM DAWKINS. GRADE 6

I realized why we couldn't see the cave from the river. There was a rock shelf right below the opening, so the cave was hidden. I pulled myself up onto the shelf, and then helped the others climb up. There were marks on the wall inside the entrance. They must have been made with a metal tool. I wondered where Milner and Ronnie were. If their raft was down below, they had to be up there somewhere.

Milner and I went over to explore the next tunnel. There were stone tablets scattered around in there, and some of them had writing on them. Milner said it looked Egyptian. He told me that the ancient Egyptians used to post warnings and curses outside their tombs. Like, anyone who disturbed the tomb would die a horrible death. I was scared, but tried not to show it. Milner said he bet we would hit the jackpot in the next tunnel.

He was right. It was the most incredible thing I had ever seen. A large room filled with mummies, dozens of them leaning against the walls in simple wooden coffins. The coffins had no tops on them, so the mummies were just standing there, staring at us. It was creepy. It looked like they were wrapped in bark or something.

On the ground were a bunch of gold swords. Gold! And in the far corner of the room was a big statue. Maybe seven feet high. A man. It looked like a Buddha sitting there. It was cross-legged, holding a flower in each hand. My flashlight shined off it. The thing was made of gold. I tapped it with my knuckles. It was solid. Solid gold. It must have been worth millions. It was beautiful.

Milner and I both cried out. I couldn't believe it! We had found the treasure of the Grand Canyon! It was ours for the taking. Milner picked up one of the swords and blew the dust off it. I'll always remember what he said to me: "Kid, guess what? You'll never have to work a day in your life. We're millionaires."

Then he took a big flask of whiskey out of his pocket, opened the top, and drank it. A little celebration. He offered me a sip, but I didn't take it. So he downed the whole thing without stopping.

While he was drinking, it crossed my mind that Milner might try something to cut me out of the deal. We didn't have any written contract or agreement. Just a handshake that said we would split anything we found down the middle.

He was bigger and stronger than me. There would be nothing to stop him from taking all the stuff for himself. In fact, there would be nothing to stop him from killing me and leaving me there. Nobody would find me for years. Maybe centuries. I'd end up like that Kinkaid guy.

I made it a point not to turn my back on Milner. Just in case. When the whiskey was finished, he threw the flask against the rocks and it shattered.

JUDY DOUGLAS. GRADE 6

I thought I heard a sound, like glass breaking. I wanted to get out of there. Just back out and climb down. The others held me and told me everything would be all right. Maybe it was just my imagination. There were some steps going up near the entrance to the cave, and we started climbing them. It was dark.

RONNIE TEOTWAWKI. GRADE 6

I heard a sound. Like footsteps. And voices. It had to be my imagination, I figured. Nobody had been in the cave for thousands of years. How could somebody be there *now*? I thought it was a zombie or something. Milner and I rushed out to the landing, the hub where G. E. Kinkaid's body was.

And that's where we saw them—Sam Dawkins, Judy, Kelsey, and Brenton. And the thing that surprised me the most was that they were with our teacher, Mr. Murphy.

KELSEY DONNELLY. GRADE 6

Well, I just screamed! Ronnie Teotwawki was standing there with that guy Milner, who had been stalking us when we had the homework machine. He was carrying a sword in his hand. And on the ground in front of them there was a dead body with no head. I had never been so terrified in my life. Judy and I screamed. I thought I might pass out.

JUDY DOUGLAS. GRADE 6

The four of us instinctively moved closer together, as a group. It just felt like a bad situation. I wished I had never come.

RONNIE TEOTWAWKI. GRADE 6

I was furious. I said to them, "What are *you* doing here?"

SAM DAWKINS. GRADE 6

So Ronnie says, "What are *you* doing here?" and I say, "The same thing you're doing here. Looking for the treasure."

RONNIE TEOTWAWKI. GRADE 6

Milner was even more mad than I was. He told them to get lost. He started yelling, "We were here first! You just followed us! You never would have found the cavern if we hadn't found it first! If anybody deserves to get the treasure, it's us. So get out!"

And he was right, too.

BRENTON DAMAGATCHI. GRADE 6

I told Ronnie that the only reason he found the cavern first was because he stole our chip and put it in his GPS.

RONNIE TEOTWAWKI. GRADE 6

I told Brenton that maybe he shouldn't have catapulted his computer into the Grand Canyon if the chip meant so much to him. There's an old law of the jungle: finders keepers. I found the chip, so it belonged to me. And I used the chip to find the treasure, so that belonged to me too.

SAM DAWKINS. GRADE 6

It was really awkward. Nobody was saying anything. Milner and Mr. Murphy were just staring at each other. Like they were really going to fight over the treasure. I looked around. There were five of us there, and only two of them. Of course, Milner had a sword in his hand, which changed the odds. And I didn't think Judy would be very useful if things were to get violent. But even so, we had the advantage.

MR. MURPHY. SIXTH-GRADE TEACHER

I could smell alcohol on Milner's breath. It was a very dangerous situation, and I felt that somebody needed to calm things down. I said that we should all be happy because we had stumbled upon a great archeological find, perhaps the most important one in American history. I pointed out that legally, any artifacts found within the Grand Canyon belong to the state of Arizona, or very possibly the Havasupai Indians, who still live on a reservation nearby. To them, this was probably sacred ground.

RONNIE TEOTWAWKI. GRADE 6

Well, Milner just flipped. He started ranting about Indians. He said, "Why is everything sacred just because some Indian touched it? They could just say the whole United States is sacred ground. They were here first. It was their land. We took it from them. We took everything from them. What's different here?"

He started waving the sword around and telling them to get out before somebody got hurt. I tried to get him to calm down, but he waved the sword at me, too. He was getting out of control. The alcohol didn't help.

MR. MURPHY. SIXTH-GRADE TEACHER

I told the kids to stand back against the wall. I had so carefully planned out this whole trip to make sure nobody would get hurt hiking, rafting, or climbing. But it never occurred to me that we would encounter a drunken lunatic with a sword. Some things you can't plan for.

SAM DAWKINS. GRADE 6

Mr. Murphy looked real calm. He kept trying to get Milner to put the sword down and talk things over man-to-man, but Milner wouldn't listen. He kept yelling and threatening us. Sometimes you can't reason with people. He was waving that sword around like he was Indiana Jones or something.

MR. MURPHY. SIXTH-GRADE TEACHER

I spent my whole career in the military.

Except for the practice range, not once did I pull the trigger on a gun. Never got into a fist-fight. Never hurt another person in my life. But I know how to defend myself. They trained me for that.

SAM DAWKINS. GRADE 6

They were circling around each other, like boxers. The only difference was that Kinkaid's dead body was between the two of them. I was paralyzed. We all were. The girls were crying and yelling for them to stop.

KELSEY DONNELLY. GRADE 6

Milner kept saying we had to leave or he'd kill us. He was crazy! Mr. Murphy kept telling him that if he put the sword down, we would leave.

BRENTON DAMAGATCHI. GRADE 6

Finally, Milner lunged at Mr. Murphy with the sword.

SAM DAWKINS. GRADE 6

Mr. Murphy kicked the sword out of his hand.

JUDY DOUGLAS. GRADE 6

The sword hit Milner on the side of his face.

KELSEY DONNELLY. GRADE 6

He put his hand to his cheek and saw the blood on it. He was real mad! He took a wild swing at Mr. Murphy with his bare fist.

MR. MURPHY. SIXTH-GRADE TEACHER

In martial arts, they teach you to use physics. If somebody lunges toward you, their forward momentum can be used to your advantage.

SAM DAWKINS. GRADE 6

Mr. Murphy ducked the punch and shoved Milner aside.

KELSEY DONNELLY. GRADE 6

Milner tripped over Kinkaid's body and lost his balance. That's when he fell down the steps.

JUDY DOUGLAS. GRADE 6

Milner went head over heels down the steps and over the rock shelf. We all ran over. His legs went over the edge.

KELSEY DONNELLY. GRADE 6

He was hanging there with his elbows up on the ledge for a moment or so.

SAM DAWKINS. GRADE 6

He was struggling to hold on.

BRENTON DAMAGATCHI. GRADE 6

He looked up at us. There was a pleading look on his face. But there was nothing we could do.

SAM DAWKINS. GRADE 6

And then he slipped off the edge.

Chapter 9

May

KELSEY DONNELLY. GRADE 6

Even now, I still can't believe it happened. It was all so fast. One second he was standing there, and the next second he was gone. May I have a tissue, please?

JUDY DOUGLAS. GRADE 6

For a moment, we were all frozen. We just stared. Like statues. Then we all rushed down the steps. Everybody was freaking out, even Mr. Murphy. And *nothing* freaks him out.

MR. MURPHY. SIXTH-GRADE TEACHER

This was not the first time I had seen a man die. But it was the first time I had seen a man die by accident. It was my fault. I was the adult in charge. I had failed. It's a failure I will have to live with for the rest of my life.

SAM DAWKINS. GRADE 6

I leaned my head over the ledge and the others held on to my legs so I wouldn't fall off. At first I didn't see anybody down there. Then I saw somebody floating in the river. Facedown. He wasn't moving. He must have hit the rocks on the way down.

BRENTON DAMAGATCHI. GRADE 6

It was my fault. I could have stopped it. I could have stepped between the two of them while they were fighting. But I froze. And in that instant, a man died. If only I had a time machine, so I could go back and erase that mistake.

KELSEY DONNELLY. GRADE 6

I hope he didn't feel too much pain. I was pretty sure he was dead. You don't survive a fall like that. It would be a miracle for him to still be alive. I said a prayer.

RONNIE TEOTWAWKI. GRADE 6

I felt really alone. The others were part of a

group. Milner was gone. Probably dead. And it was my fault. I was the one who brought him in on the treasure hunt. If I hadn't, he would still be alive today.

JUDY DOUGLAS. GRADE 6

I was crying. He wasn't a nice man. I didn't like the guy or anything. But even so, you don't want to see that happen to anybody. I had never even been to a funeral before, and now—in the space of a few minutes—I had seen one dead man, and another man die. I was in shock. We all were. We just sat there silently for a long time.

RONNIE TEOTWAWKI. GRADE 6

What should we do? That's what we were all asking. My first thought was that we should keep our mouths shut. I didn't want to tell anyone else what happened. Nobody else had to know. Nobody could tie us to Milner.

But I realized that was stupid. The police were eventually going to find Milner's van parked at Lee's Ferry. Somebody was going to find his raft. People had probably seen me meeting with him at the visitor center. Somebody would report him missing. And I was sure that one of the others would spill the beans. They're all so honest. They wouldn't know how to tell a lie if their lives depended on it.

MR. MURPHY, SIXTH-GRADE TEACHER

There was no question in my mind what we had to do. We needed to alert the police right away. I'm not just saying that because I'm sitting in a police station. It was the right thing to do.

RONNIE TEOTWAWKI, GRADE 6

When Mr. Murphy said we had to notify the police, I didn't argue.

JUDY DOUGLAS, GRADE 6

I don't know why we did it, but we all hugged. Even Ronnie. He was part of our group now too. He was a jerk and all, but he had been through it just like us.

When I first met Kelsey and Snik, I didn't like them either. But we had been through a lot together with the homework machine, and we became best friends.

Mr. Murphy took out his cell phone to call the police, but he couldn't get a signal.

BRENTON DAMAGATCHI. GRADE 6

I went over to Ronnie and told him to give me the GPS. I didn't ask him, I told him. And he gave it to me. I opened it up right there and pulled out the chip. The little red light was still attached to it, and it was blinking. It's amazing that such a tiny thing could cause so much trouble. I put the chip in my pocket. I gave the GPS back to Ronnie.

KELSEY DONNELLY. GRADE 6

Snik said that we should agree on our story so we would all say the same thing to you police folks. Well, we jumped all over him. What story? We had no story. We would just tell the truth. What happened to Milner was an accident. He was crazy. He would be fine today if he hadn't gone loco and started swinging that sword around. Mr. Murphy did what he had to do to protect us from getting hurt.

SAM DAWKINS. GRADE 6

They were all mad at me just because I used the word "story." I didn't mean we should *lie* about what happened. I just wanted us to be consistent so nobody would get into any trouble.

One thing was amazing to me. The one person who wasn't sure that telling the truth was the
right thing to do was Mr. Murphy.

BRENTON DAMAGATCHI. GRADE 6

Mr. Murphy said we should tell the truth, of
course, but not necessarily the *whole* truth. He
said that if the police found out that he fought
with Milner and threw him down those steps,
they might decide that a crime had been com-
mitted. And if Milner turned up dead, the crime
would be murder. It made a certain amount of
sense—at the time, anyway.

SAM DAWKINS. GRADE 6

I thought Mr. Murphy was right. What
purpose would it serve to tell everybody there
was this big fight and that he threw Milner
down the steps?

We could just say we saw a body floating
down the river. That was the truth. I *did* see a
body floating down the river. Leave it at that.
People fall off the cliffs in the Grand Canyon all
the time, right? Milner could have been one of
those guys who liked to pee off high places. Or

maybe he was getting his picture taken and took a few too many steps back. After all, Ronnie said Milner was drinking. If the body was found, there would be alcohol in his bloodstream.

RONNIE TEOTWAWKI, GRADE 6

We shook hands on it. I thought that would be the end of it.

JUDY DOUGLAS, GRADE 6

I didn't feel good about what we decided. We saw more than just a man floating in the river. We saw a man get out of control with a weapon, and we saw Mr. Murphy disarm him. In the process, the man fell down the steps and over the ledge. *That's* what we saw.

I'm not very good at lying. And withholding the whole truth is not that different from lying. Some people can stare you right in the face and say something they know isn't true. I don't want to be one of those people, but I wish I could do that sometimes.

RONNIE TEOTWAWKI, GRADE 6

We were about to climb down when I

remembered something—the treasure. They hadn't even seen it yet. I took them into the room where the Buddha and all that other gold stuff was.

SAM DAWKINS. GRADE 6

It was amazing. Just amazing. Like a museum carved into the rock. I never saw so much gold before. I couldn't really appreciate it though, because of what had just happened with Milner.

JUDY DOUGLAS. GRADE 6

We didn't know what to do about it. Should we take some of that stuff with us to prove we found it? Leave it? Contact the historical society when we got back? It was Ronnie, of all people, who came up with the best idea.

RONNIE TEOTWAWKI. GRADE 6

I said we should forget about the treasure. Don't tell anybody about it. Just leave it there for some future generation to discover. The treasure was nothing but bad luck anyway. Maybe it was cursed, like the tomb of King Tut. That Kinkaid guy discovered the treasure, and he was dead. Now Milner was dead. I didn't want anybody else to die. We all just wanted to get out of there.

MR. MURPHY. SIXTH-GRADE TEACHER

We climbed down from the cavern and started making our way back. As soon as my cell phone was able to get a signal, I called police headquarters and reported that we had seen a body floating in the river. That's all I said. When the officer asked me if I could give her any details, I said no.

It was stupid. I feel terrible about it. I apologize. It was wrong to deceive you folks. But I hope you believe me that what happened was an accident.

POLICE CHIEF REBECCA FISH: LOG BOOK

May 1, 11:23 a.m.: Gerald Murphy, teacher at Grand Canyon School, reports body floating in Colorado River downstream from Bright Angel Campground.

May 1, 9:12 p.m.: Found white van parked after hours in lot at Lee's Ferry. Arizona plate #SDF759. Registered in the name of Richard Milner.

JUDY DOUGLAS. GRADE 6

We went back to school the next day, and nobody said anything. I think I was still in shock. We just glanced at each other nervously. But I knew that I would never be the same person after what happened. I felt like I wasn't a kid anymore. I had seen somebody die.

SAM DAWKINS. GRADE 6

I didn't even know Milner, but I had the same feeling as when my dad died. Like a part of me was missing. I started watching the news on TV to see if Milner's body turned up. I mean, it was floating in the river. At some point it would wash up against the rocks and somebody would find it. But there was nothing about it in the newspaper or on TV. They just had all these reports about Canyonist nuts wandering around because the end of the world was coming.

POLICE CHIEF REBECCA FISH

The tourist season don't usually start up around here till school lets out and people take their vacations. But in the beginnin' of May, these lunatics were just streamin' into the park in droves. I never seen anything like it! They all had

144

this glassy look in their eyes. When you talked to 'em, they'd just say the world was gonna end on Mother's Day, and they wanted to be here.

It got to be a real problem. You'd be walkin' down the street and there would be three of 'em standing on their heads, and chanting. Folks would complain. But what was I supposed to do? I couldn't arrest these loonies. There's no law against standin' on your head in public. Maybe there should be.

BRENTON DAMAGATCHI. GRADE 6

I had wiped the website clean as soon as I saw that people didn't realize Canyonism was a joke. But it didn't make any difference. The crazies had printed out the whole website and made copies of it to give to their friends. They would walk around reading it like it was the Bible.

KELSEY DONNELLY. GRADE 6

We only had a few more weeks of school left. Nobody had found Milner's body. We began to relax and stop thinking about him all the time. Even if they found Milner, I figured there was no way anyone would know we had anything to do with his death.

JUDY DOUGLAS. GRADE 6

We were a little team now. Not just the four of us. Mr. Murphy and Ronnie were part of the team too. Because we knew a secret that nobody else knew. It wasn't a good feeling. Not for me, anyway. I wanted to tell somebody. Anybody.

SAM DAWKINS. GRADE 6

I was keeping an eye on Brenton. When we were using the homework machine, he was the one who couldn't keep his mouth shut. If he hadn't spilled the beans, we would probably still be using it today to do our homework. We never would have catapulted the computer into the Grand Canyon. None of this other stuff would have happened. Brenton isn't good at keeping secrets.

BRENTON DAMAGATCHI. GRADE 6

I had no intention of telling anyone the full story of what happened to Milner in that cave. I had put it behind me. But something else was weighing on my mind—the chip. I had been carrying it around in my pocket ever since I got it back from Ronnie. I didn't want it out of my sight. It had caused too much damage. In the wrong hands, it could do a lot more. I decided that we had to get rid of it once and for all.

BRENTON'S MOM

Brenton told me that a few of his friends were coming over after school. And their teacher, Mr. Murphy, too. I had met him on Back to School Night, and he seemed very nice. I made cookies.

KELSEY DONNELLY. GRADE 6

We all went over to Brenton's house for a meeting. He took us down in the basement and we sat around the Ping-Pong table. Then he took out the computer chip and put it on the table in front of us. That blinking red light was still attached to it. I hated that thing.

JUDY DOUGLAS. GRADE 6

Brenton said we had to get rid of the chip, and we all agreed. Even Ronnie. The question was, how would we do it? Catapulting it into the Grand Canyon obviously didn't work the first time. Everybody had an idea.

SAM DAWKINS. GRADE 6

I said we should just crush it. I could smash that sucker with a sledgehammer in a second. Bam! No problem. Done. But nobody liked my idea. I don't know why. Usually simple solutions are the best ones.

KELSEY DONNELLY. GRADE 6

I've been to this website called "Will It Blend?" This guy with a high-powered kitchen blender takes everyday objects and sees if he can chop them up into tiny little pieces. So he takes, like, a baseball. Or a cell phone. And he blends it. It's cool. I suggested we try to blend the chip. But nobody wanted to ruin their blender.

SAM DAWKINS. GRADE 6

People were suggesting that we flush it down a toilet, bury it underground, burn it in a campfire, all kinds of crazy stuff. I remembered one of those *Terminator* movies, where these machines take over the world and decide they're gonna get rid of the human race. Every time the good guys think they kill one of their cyborg assassins, it finds a way to come back to life. We were gonna have to come up with a foolproof method of getting rid of the chip forever.

JUDY DOUGLAS, GRADE 6

It seemed to me that the right thing to do would be to turn the computer chip over to the police and let them figure out what to do with it. They would know a way to dispose of it safely. But everybody started yelling at me. They all said that if the authorities got ahold of a chip this powerful, they would use it to create some super weapon and start another war or spy on American citizens. They may have been right. I don't know.

BRENTON DAMAGATCHI, GRADE 6

I casually mentioned that I wished there was some way to make the chip disappear. Just get it off this planet so it would never hurt anyone again. Well, Snik got this gleam in his eye and instantly I knew what he was thinking. Both of us had the same idea, almost at the same time.

SAM DAWKINS, GRADE 6

We could build a rocket. We could shoot the chip into space. It was brilliant! Genius!

MR. MURPHY. SIXTH-GRADE TEACHER

I was against the idea. Building a rocket is expensive, time-consuming, and dangerous. There's a good chance you can have a misfire. What if the thing lands in a populated area? Or on somebody's house?

They begged me. Snik and Brenton actually got down on their knees. I thought it over and decided we had no other choice. We had to get rid of that chip. And the safest way to get rid of it permanently would be to shoot it into space.

KELSEY DONNELLY. GRADE 6

The boys got all excited at the idea of shooting the chip out of the Earth's atmosphere in a rocket. It didn't seem possible to me. But Mr. Murphy spent, like, his whole career working for NASA. So he knew what to do.

MR. MURPHY. SIXTH-GRADE TEACHER

The question is, where does the Earth's atmosphere end and space begin? There's no precise answer. It's not like there's a strict border line, like on a map between two countries.

But most people don't realize how thin the atmosphere is. The planet is sort of like a human cell, and the atmosphere is like the protective membrane around it.

JUDY DOUGLAS. GRADE 6

Mr. Murphy told us there are traces of oxygen and nitrogen a hundred miles up. But almost all of our atmosphere is the troposphere, which is only about seven miles above the surface of the Earth.

SAM DAWKINS. GRADE 6

Seven miles? Who knew? No wonder people like Kelsey get so worked up about pollution and climate change. A seven-mile layer of protection surrounding the planet didn't sound like very much. I always thought it was like fifty miles at least.

KELSEY DONNELLY. GRADE 6

So if we could build a rocket that would fly seven miles up, we could get the chip out of the Earth's atmosphere. It was the only way.

Ha! Talk about rocket science!

BRENTON DAMAGATCHI, GRADE 6

When I was little, I used to read books about the space program all the time. I remember that when a spaceship returns to Earth, it has to enter our atmosphere at a very precise angle. If it doesn't, it will either burn up during reentry or bounce off the atmosphere and float into space. So if we could get a rocket—with our chip inside—above the atmosphere, chances are it would float away or burst into flames upon reentry. And either one would be fine with us, because we just wanted to get rid of the chip.

SAM DAWKINS, GRADE 6

Part of me was thinking that if we wanted the chip to burn up, why don't we just stick the thing in a microwave oven and set it on "popcorn"? You know? Or just melt it with a magnifying glass. That would be a lot easier. But the idea of building a rocket with Mr. Murphy—who spent years working for NASA—sounded cool, so I said let's do it.

POLICE CHIEF REBECCA FISH: LOG BOOK

May 5: Call from New Jersey hiker named

Herbert Dunn. Saw a body floating near Glen Canyon Dam. Sent Officers Kommedal and Levin to conduct preliminary investigation.

KELSEY DONNELLY. GRADE 6

We all went over to Mr. Murphy's house—or his garage, really—to start building the rocket. I wasn't much help. Mr. Murphy and Brenton were like real rocket scientists. They were talking about all this stuff like ion propulsion and pounds of thrust that made no sense at all. I never realized that rockets don't have wings like planes because the wings only help at low speeds. Once you get moving really fast, wings would just create more air resistance.

BRENTON DAMAGATCHI. GRADE 6

Mr. Murphy had it all worked out. He has been building rockets all his life, and he gave me a crash course. Basically, you need to shoot liquid hydrogen and liquid oxygen into a combustion chamber really fast, and ignite them. When the hot gases produced by the combustion shoot out through the nozzle, it produces thrust. The more fuel, the more thrust. The more thrust, the higher you fly. That's how a liquid-fueled rocket works. It's simple, really.

KELSEY DONNELLY. GRADE 6

We worked really hard on the rocket. Brenton and Mr. Murphy did all the thinking and planning. The rest of us—me, Snik, Ronnie, and Judy—did the grunt work. Screwing in screws, getting materials they needed, picking up pizza and Chinese food to keep them going.

POLICE CHIEF REBECCA FISH: LOG BOOK

May 6: The body that washed up at Glen Canyon Dam is Richard Milner, the guy whose van was found in the parking lot at Lee's Ferry. Alcohol in bloodstream. Possible suicide. No note.

SAM DAWKINS. GRADE 6

The rocket was coming along good. Mr. Murphy knows everything about aerodynamics and propulsion and stuff. Some of his old NASA buddies helped him get his hands on this special rocket fuel that is, like, totally powerful and you need top secret security clearance to get near it. This is the stuff they used to launch the space

154

shuttle. We had to have that fuel to get the rocket as high as it needed to go.

BRENTON DAMAGATCHI. GRADE 6

Maybe this would be the solution to a lot of our waste problems, it occurred to me. Instead of filling up landfills, why can't we just shoot our garbage into outer space? Get rid of it entirely. The same thing with pollution, spent nuclear fuel, and the exhaust from coal-burning power plants. We should just put that stuff in a rocket once a month, and shoot it to the moon. It seems to me that if we can land a man on the moon, we can dump our garbage there.

POLICE CHIEF REBECCA FISH: LOG BOOK

May 7: Looks like that Milner fella did not just fall into the river. Cut marks on left cheek could only have been made by a sharp blade. I don't think the guy cut himself shaving. Looks like there mighta been a struggle.

Called Gerald Murphy, the teacher who spotted the body floating in the river. Not home. Left message.

POLICE CHIEF REBECCA FISH: LOG BOOK

May 8: Murphy did not return call. Left another message. May have to go out to his house in person.

JUDY DOUGLAS, GRADE 6

Mr. Murphy seemed like he was in a big hurry to finish building the rocket. He wouldn't tell us why. We were working on it every night. Only later did we learn the police had found Milner's body and they were trying to reach Mr. Murphy to question him about it. He wasn't returning the calls. He was probably afraid he'd be sent to jail, and he wanted to get the rocket launched first.

SAM DAWKINS, GRADE 6

Finally we finished building the rocket. It was the middle of May, I guess.

BRENTON'S MOM

I was a little bit upset because it was Mother's Day, and he didn't get me anything. Usually, Brenton will make me a card or something. But all he seemed to care about was some top secret project he and his friends were working on. He wouldn't tell me what it was.

RONNIE TEOTWAWKI. GRADE 6

It was a Sunday morning. We wheeled the rocket out of Mr. Murphy's garage and into the field behind his house. It wasn't some cheap plastic model rocket, mind you. This one was as tall as I am, and heavy.

JUDY DOUGLAS. GRADE 6

We set the rocket up on a slab of concrete in the middle of the field. I guess there had been a swing set there a long time ago.

SAM DAWKINS. GRADE 6

A bunch of those Canyonist nutcases were wandering around, like always. Some of them saw our rocket, and they started walking over, real slow. It was like *Night of the Living Dead*, with those zombies walking toward us.

JUDY DOUGLAS. GRADE 6

One of them says to me, "Will this rocket take us to another world when the Earth explodes?" I mean, really!

BRENTON DAMAGATCHI. GRADE 6

Everybody was telling me to hurry up and

launch the rocket before one of those Canyonists got too close and damaged it. I opened the door of the nose cone, and inserted the chip with the little red light. It was sad, in a way. I didn't want to see it go. But we had to get rid of it. "So long, old friend," I said to it. We've gotta do what we've gotta do.

SAM DAWKINS. GRADE 6

One of those nutcases comes over to us and asks if we know anybody named Brenton. So I pointed to Brenton.

BRENTON DAMAGATCHI. GRADE 6

They all got down on their knees in a semi-circle around me and started chanting "Notnerb! It is the immortal Notnerb spelled backward! At last we have found you. You are our savior!" and all this stuff. They were thanking me for the weight they lost and frequent-flyer miles they won. It was insane. I tried to tell them that Canyonism was just a joke, but they wouldn't listen. They were praying to me.

KELSEY DONNELLY. GRADE 6

Suddenly a cop car pulled up and you got out. We were all yelling at Brenton, "Hurry up!

The cops are here! We gotta get this baby up in the air!"

JUDY DOUGLAS. GRADE 6

All these Canyonists started eating Twinkies and chanting, "Life began here! It will end here! Life began here! It will end here!" They were creepy.

RONNIE TEOTWAWKI. GRADE 6

That's when you went over to Mr. Murphy and started questioning him. I heard you say, "The body of a man named Richard Milner turned up at Glen Canyon. Is there anything you want to tell me, Mr. Murphy?"

SAM DAWKINS. GRADE 6

So Mr. Murphy says, "One minute, officer," and you said, "Not one minute. Now!"

MR. MURPHY. SIXTH-GRADE TEACHER

I was yelling at everybody, "Back away from the rocket! This is very dangerous!"

BRENTON DAMAGATCHI. GRADE 6

The Canyonists were telling everybody that the world was going to end, and that I predicted it.

JUDY DOUGLAS, GRADE 6

They were yelling that the aliens will return and only the Canyonists will be saved.

KELSEY DONNELLY, GRADE 6

That's when you said to Mr. Murphy, "You got a permit for that thing? We got laws against firing off explosives so close to a national park."

RONNIE TEOTWAWKI, GRADE 6

As all this was happening, a black car pulled up and four Japanese guys wearing trenchcoats got out. They were coming over to us, saying they wanted their computer chip back. I remembered Milner told me that some gangsters were after him.

JUDY DOUGLAS, GRADE 6

I was yelling, "Hurry!"

MR. MURPHY, SIXTH-GRADE TEACHER

I shouted, "Stand back!"

RONNIE TEOTWAWKI, GRADE 6

I said, "Don't we have to have a countdown?"

SAM DAWKINS. GRADE 6

So I say, "No time for a countdown! Just fire it!"

JUDY DOUGLAS. GRADE 6

The Canyonists were coming from all over, and another police car pulled up, and those gangsters were coming toward us, and everybody was yelling and shouting at each other. I just covered my ears.

BRENTON DAMAGATCHI. GRADE 6

And I pushed the button.

Chapter 10

Afterward

SAM DAWKINS. GRADE 6

So, that's pretty much what happened. You guys saw the rocket go up. Man, it was a beautiful thing! Everybody just stopped yelling and looked up. Then they were all clapping. The rocket just kept going and going. Finally, we lost sight of it. It never came down, at least not anywhere around here. I have to assume it made it out of the atmosphere.

BRENTON DAMAGATCHI. GRADE 6

And for all we know, that little red light is up there in outer space right now, floating around, still blinking away.

Note:

Much of the information about the Grand
Canyon was found in *Over the Edge: Death in
Grand Canyon*, by Michael P. Ghiglieri and
Thomas M. Myers (Puma Press, 2001). I also
used *The Lonely Planet Grand Canyon National
Park Guidebook* and *Frommer's Grand Canyon
National Park*.

About the Author

In addition to *The Homework Machine*, Dan Gutman is the author of many books for kids, such as *Nightmare at the Book Fair*, *Getting Air*, *Race for the Sky*, *Back in Time with Thomas Edison*, *The Kid Who Ran for President*, *Honus and Me*, *The Million Dollar Shot* and the My Weird School series. To find out more about Dan and his books, visit dangutman.com.